The Closed Loop:
Implementing Activity-Based Planning and Budgeting

The Closed Loop:
Implementing Activity-Based Planning and Budgeting

Editors:
Stephen C. Hansen
The George Washington University / University of California at Los Angeles

Robert G. Torok
IBM Business Consulting Services

Authors:

Alan Stratton (chair) - *SAS Institute*

Gerry Brennan - *Emerson Electric*

Rollin D. Brewster III - *US Marine Corps*

Lanelle Butts - *US Army*

Martin Croxton - *BearingPoint*

Stephen C. Hansen - *GWU/UCLA*

Paul Legler - *Grant Thornton, LLP*

Arlene Minkiewicz - *PRICE Systems, L.L.C.*

Jack Niemiec - *US Coast Guard*

Pedro San Martin - *IBM Business Consulting Services*

Derek Sandison - *INTEGRATED International Business Consulting, Inc.*

Mike Shirk - *US Coast Guard*

Mark Stevens - *PCS Consulting, Inc.*

Robert G. Torok - *IBM Business Consulting Services*

Paul Trampert - *Grant Thornton, LLP*

Contributors:

Ron Bleeker - *CAM-I / Northrop Grumman*

Al Cato - *US Army*

Capt Joe Crance - *US Air Force*

Paul Dierks - *Wake Forest University (retired)*

Norm Frause - *Boeing*

Todd Geiser - *PRICE Systems, L.L.C.*

Elisabeth McDonald - *GATX*

Capt Andy Meek - *US Air Force*

Paul Morgan - *ALG Software*

Patti Norman - *Honeywell*

Mike Novak - *DaimlerChrysler*

Steve Player - *The Player Group*

Roman Rapp - *SAP AG*

Steve Schreck - *Boeing*

Laura Zander - *Naval Postgraduate School/MEVATEC*

**Consortium for Advanced
Manufacturing - International**

6737 Brentwood Stair Road, Suite 214
Ft. Worth, TX 76112

ISBN: 1-59453-166-8

Bookman Publishing
Martinsville, Indiana

EXECUTIVE SUMMARY

Budgeting is an important management control system in many organizations.[1] Its main goals are to facilitate operational planning, resource allocation, performance evaluation, strategy formation, communication, and benchmarking.[2] However, budgeting can be a frustrating management process. The traditional budgeting process is broadly seen as having many flaws or limitations, the chief ones being that it:

- Is too time consuming,

- Requires too many iterations,

- Can be very costly,

- Does not address capacity,

- Is based on an extrapolation of prior period data,

- Is influenced by political gaming, and

- Receives limited buy-in or acceptance of results.

---

[1] Simons, R. 1995. *Levers of Control: How Managers Use Innovative Control Systems to Drive Strategic Renewal*. Boston, MA: HBS Press.

[2] Hansen, S., and W. A. Van der Stede. 2002. Six Facets of Budgeting: Antecedents and Performance. Working Paper, University of Southern California.

The Activity-Based Planning and Budgeting (ABPB) Interest Group of the Consortium for Advanced Manufacturing – International (CAM-I) was formed to investigate how to improve planning and budgeting by incorporating activity-based concepts. This book contains the Group's recommended approach:

- The **CAM-I ABPB Closed-Loop Model**, (referred to as "the Closed-Loop Model"), a new approach to calculating the activity, resource, and financial requirements of an organization and its units,[3]

- The **CAM-I ABPB Process**, which contains the business processes and techniques needed to support the Closed-Loop Model, and

- The **CAM-I ABPB Implementation Program**, a structured approach to introducing the Closed-Loop Model and ABPB Process into an organization.

The three parts of this book build on each other, starting with the development and application of the Closed-Loop Model, then its implementation and sustainment, and finally the linkage of the Closed-Loop Model with traditional approaches and other strategic initiatives.

---

[3] Throughout this book, the term "organization" refers to the highest level of a corporation or agency, such as the parent company. The term "unit" refers to any group in the organization, such as a subsidiary, branch, division, or department.

The heart of the recommended approach is a budget calculation engine, the ABPB Closed-Loop Model, which is summarized in Figure 1. The Closed-Loop Model has three important features.

- It is activity based,

- It explicitly matches resource demand and resource capacity, and

- It achieves operational balance and then confirms financial balance.

The detailed calculations involved in the Closed-Loop Model are shown in Figure 2. The Closed-Loop Model is based on an integrated view of the organization and solves many of the problems of most traditional budgeting approaches. The Closed-Loop Model explicitly links resource capacity with resource demand and avoids building a budget based solely on extrapolation of prior data. Because the Closed-Loop Model is based on an observable model, there is less room for disagreement on many of the operating and financial factors, thus reducing political gaming. When staff and management can observe the relationship between inputs and outputs, they are more likely to buy into the budgeting process. Finally, because the Closed-Loop Model is rooted in the actual operating and financial performance of the organization, budget iterations will cost less, will be more meaningful, and will be fewer in number (if management does not use the improved planning

Figure 1: Overview of the CAM-I ABPB Closed-Loop Model

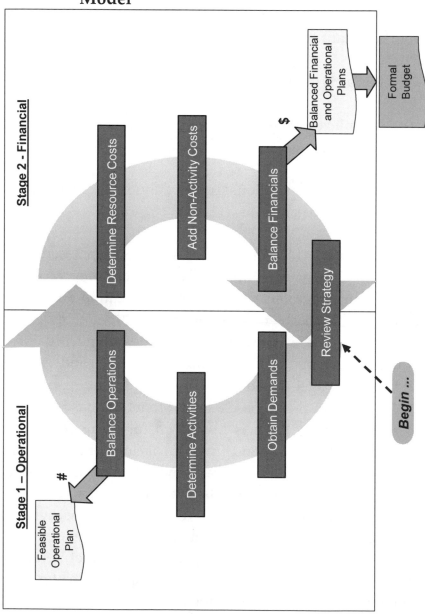

Figure 2: The CAM-I ABPB Closed-Loop Model

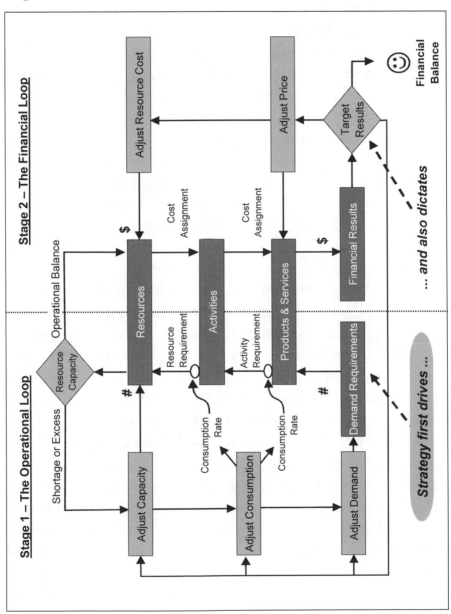

features to run more scenarios).

This book contains many examples of applications of the Closed-Loop Model in a variety of industries. For competitive and confidentiality reasons, none of the organizations have been named, although the concepts and lessons learned are incorporated throughout.

While this book is intended for managers and executives with responsibilities for organizational budgets, we firmly expect that managers in operating functions will find the Closed-Loop Model as useful as those in financial functions.

But why read this book? After all, in today's literature, one finds strong advocates of simply eliminating the periodic budgeting process and the detailed budget which results. We do not believe that such a solution is either viable or practical for the overwhelming majority of organizations, and therefore the budget is likely here to stay.

The Closed-Loop Model reflects a powerful new budgeting approach that speaks to many of the problems associated with traditional budgets and budget processes while retaining and enhancing the benefits obtained from the process. At a minimum, the Closed-Loop Model can supply an improved calculation engine for, and extend the operational relevance of, a traditional budget process. However, an organization will only obtain the full benefit of using the Closed-Loop Model by restructuring the performance evaluation system so that the operating and financial metrics are in harmony with those used for performance measurement. Following that path will also support an organization as it strives to improve the integrity and accuracy of its financial planning and budgeting processes, an integral component in performance measurement and reporting.

This book provides guidance for achieving the maximum benefit from the budget process.

FOREWORD

Organization and management ideas and practices have advanced considerably for many years. But the art of management is in its infancy. Developing our knowledge, skills, and attitudes begins in books like this one. The foundations of general management are explored here. How? By focusing on planning and budgeting fundamentals. By building a Closed-Loop Model that provides more rigor and relevance for improving management's knowledge of facts and relationships that should improve decision-making. In short, this book prompts readers to think more deeply about how to run organizations. Moreover, this book covers detailed implementation of the methods that it favors.

Do you think that your organization's planning and budgeting can be improved? Budgets have their fans and their attackers. Nevertheless, everybody agrees that such planning tools are imperfect. Some researchers and managers, including the authors of this book, believe that improvements can be made. Others believe that budgets should be abandoned altogether. The accompanying ferment in the literature and at conferences underscores that we all have plenty to learn about the basics of management.

The Closed Loop identifies the strengths and the numerous problems of budgeting and then develops a model of planning and budgeting. The Closed-Loop Model is an activity-based algorithm that achieves operational balance, then financial balance, and explicitly matches resource demand and resource capacity. The model's approach explicitly emphasizes and links operational performance with financial results. It reviews an organization's strategy and pinpoints the roles of demand, consumption, and capacity in operations. In doing so, the model focuses on the demands for products and services, their activity requirements, their resource requirements, their capacity requirements, and their interrelationships. The model heavily uses activity-based concepts and capacity concepts, bringing them down to the activity and resource levels. Particularly noteworthy is how the authors weave capacity analysis and measures into the Closed-Loop Model.

The Closed Loop has a common thread that has persisted in management accounting for more than a hundred years: The attempts to link causes and effects. Examples include the increasingly granulated or refined approaches toward allocations of indirect costs to products, services, and customers. For example, in manufacturing companies the procession has been from broadly averaged, plant-wide overhead rates, to departmental rates, to narrower, microscopic rates based on activities within departments, each rate tied to a different cost driver. Other examples are various versions of the balanced scorecard. All of them center on the idea of leading and lagging measures of performance.

A unifying underpinning of the Closed-Loop Model is its focus on cause-effect relationships, on identifying leading and lagging measures. That is why the operational loop and its non-financial results play the leading roles in the model. The financial loop represents the lagging measures. To predict financial results more accurately, managers must have confidence in their predictions of operational metrics. To enhance accuracy, better data must be gathered regarding the relationships of demand, consumption, and capacity. Fortunately, information technology has progressed so that details can be collected more economically than ever. Therefore, the demands for more accurate linking of causes and effects are now more easily satisfied.

Systems, tools, and techniques, including the Closed-Loop Model, are economic goods, just like beer or milk. Consumers buy enough beer or milk to satisfy their perceived wants – and no more. Similarly, managers buy enough sophistication in their methods and systems – and no more. The authors of this book recognize that management decisions regarding costs and benefits will affect the feasibility of adopting the Closed-Loop Model.

The Closed Loop is the result of thorough thinking about both concepts and practical difficulties of implementation. The model is clearly presented, including its necessary details and possible problems. This work is the product of many minds working together. It will appeal especially to readers who are not satisfied with glib coinage of new terms and vague generalizations. It provides an in-depth innovative model for improving planning, budgeting, and general management.

Charles T. Horngren
Stanford University

A WORD FROM THE PUBLISHER

CAM-I has been at the leading edge of developments in the field of cost management for over 20 years. We have been at the forefront of knowledge in Activity-Based Costing and Activity-Based Management for as long as the concepts have existed, and have been involved in methodology development for almost as long. Our work has extended our "cost" body of knowledge into related fields such as capacity measurement and process management.

All of these efforts and developments have focused on business information and approaches that assessed the past or present. But the future is now! On behalf of CAM-I and our member organizations, I am very proud to publish our first book distinctly focused on business processes that look way down the road, not in the mirror or to the next traffic sign.

No one has truly addressed the fundamental problems that vex one of the most troubling business processes of the day: the period (usually annual) budget. Many have tried approaches that simplify, streamline, or speed up the budget process but all of these ideas continue to be built on the same foundation as the current process. We believe that there is a better way.

This book applies much of the knowledge that CAM-I has developed over the past two decades, fully leveraging the principles of ABC and extending them to incorporate capacity measures and process management. And its sole objective is to help you and your organization plan and budget for the future. Activity-Based Planning and Budgeting (ABPB) drives organizations to use the information and data they already have in a way not seen before: to make educated and testable predictions about future business requirements and results. And this approach does so in a way that truly streamlines the budget process, removing much of the political gaming that invariably goes on.

I encourage you to read this and take its ideas to heart. Not only do we provide the methodology, but we have also shown numerous examples of its application in different settings and provided the reader with an implementation framework to guide you through the process. I trust you will find it as valuable as our members already have.

On behalf of CAM-I, I would like to thank the many people who have helped to bring this book to fruition.

- Professor David Keys of Northern Illinois University and Mr. Pat Dowdle of Process Advantage provided invaluable comments with their wisdom, insight, and experiences as the manuscript reached its final stages.

- The SAS Institute was extremely generous in providing us with the services of Ms. Debbie Willmschen as an editor, to help us with language, grammar, flow, and form.

- IBM allowed us to "draw" on Mr. Adam Dobrer to make our many figures tell the story.

- Nancy Thomas and the staff of CAM-I kept us on track and helped us complete the project in a timely fashion.

- And finally, Professor Charles Horngren of Stanford University, who took the time not only to write the Foreword to this book but also read the manuscript in its entirety, making incisive comments and improvements throughout.

Our co-editors, Stephen Hansen and Robert Torok, would still be toiling at these tasks if not for the assistance of Debbie, SAS, Adam, and IBM.

Ron Bleeker
CAM-I / Northrop Grumman

TABLE OF CONTENTS

PART 1: THE ACTIVITY-BASED PLANNING AND BUDGETING CLOSED-LOOP MODEL

PART 3: DERIVING VALUE FROM THE ACTIVITY-BASED PLANNING AND BUDGETING PROCESS

FIGURES AND TABLES

Chapter 3

Chapter 4

Chapter 5

Chapter 7

Chapter 8

Chapter 9

Chapter 10

Chapter 11

Chapter 12

Chapter 13

Chapter 14

PART 1

THE ACTIVITY-BASED PLANNING AND BUDGETING CLOSED-LOOP MODEL

1 CHAPTER

A New Approach

Many people view an organization's budget as a set of numbers given from on high, something mysterious that they receive but into which they have little or no input.

While the budget may not be definitive and is certainly not carved in stone, it was originally designed to add value to the organization.

A value-adding budget process is possible. This book introduces a new, more rational approach to budgeting with the hope that it can help organizations successfully develop and implement useful budgets. Our approach has been successfully applied in multiple organizations by many authors of this book. Elements have been implemented in the transportation, consumer products, utility, and manufacturing industries, in a shared services setting in the military, and in a branch of the United States Department of Justice.[4] The CAM-I ABPB Interest Group believes that the concept and approach described here is the most significant advancement in the field of Planning and Budgeting in the past thirty years.

This chapter presents the organizational benefits of budgeting, then turns to challenges with current budgeting practices, describes the essence of this new approach, shows which challenges this new budgeting approach can and cannot overcome, describes the basic knowledge level required for the approach, and provides a roadmap for the remainder of the book.

1.1 THE ORGANIZATIONAL VALUE OF BUDGETING AND THE BUDGET PROCESS

The budget and the budgeting process are essential to any well-run organization. Budgets and the budgeting process can play many different roles.

The budget can provide **an organization-wide, coordinated plan** for acquiring resources and producing outputs. The budget informs all units of the organization on how each one fits into the overall structure, what each needs to make, sell, or support throughout the period (most

---

[4] Confidentiality agreements preclude the disclosure of the names of the organizations.

commonly one year), and at what cost.

The budget can provide **a benchmark for judging manager and unit performance**. A well-developed budget captures what the organization expects to happen during the coming period and can serve as a performance target that managers wish to achieve.

The budget can serve as a **means of identifying the impact of unexpected occurrences**. Comparing the actual results to the budgeted (expected) results identifies the magnitude of the impact of unexpected occurrences and may also provide information about the origin of such events.

The budget can **help allocate resources and funds across units**. Organizations often use expected profits and cash flows from each unit to decide which will receive more or less resources in the coming period. This resource allocation frequently covers both operating as well as capital resources. Many organizations will make mid-period adjustments to planned resource allocations based on reporting units' performance relative to budget in the first part of a given budget period.

A budget can **communicate an organization's goals to its employees**. The budget encompasses a set of agreed upon assumptions over what should happen in the coming fiscal period and is a visible guideline of strategic intent that everyone can see and use as a reference. Furthermore, the budget process provides a reality check on an organization's strategy, since the budget process requires an organization to generate a feasible plan to achieve the strategic goals. If the strategic plan is flawed, a sound budget process will reveal the underlying problems, particularly when comparing budgets to targets set through the strategic planning process.[5]

The budget may be used as **an authorization for employees to spend money**. In many settings (particularly government ones), managers need a document providing them with the legal right to spend money, and the approved budget often serves that purpose. The budget provides a list of how and on what a manager can — and, equally important, cannot — spend money.

The budget can be an important **power-affirming ritual**. The budget process can settle the question of who is in charge and the limits of their authority and responsibility.

This is a list of noble roles. The problems arise in achieving them.

1.2 THE CHALLENGES FACING TRADITIONAL BUDGETING PRACTICES

The challenges facing traditional budgeting practices are well–known and widely accepted. For example, Larry

---

[5] A sound budget process can only identify those errors that drive extreme operational results and which managers are willing to reconsider in light of the operational and financial requirements. For example, a traditional budget based on a strategic plan that calls for a 20% increase in volume will not identify the fact that such a volume increase requires an increase in resources far beyond the organization's capabilities. In contrast, the approach described in this book, the Closed-Loop Model, is designed to highlight these operating requirements and thus the potential infeasibility of the budget.

Bossidy and Ram Charan recently wrote:[6]

> We see three major flaws in the budgeting or
> operations process at most companies.   First, the
> process doesn't provide for robust dialogue on the
> plan's assumptions.   Second, the budget is built
> around the results that top management wants, but it
> doesn't discuss or specify the action programs that
> will make those outcomes a reality.   Third, the
> process doesn't provide coaching opportunities for
> people to learn the totality of the business ... **the
> budget should be the financial expression of the
> operating plan** [emphasis added]...

The words "the budget is built around the results that
top management wants" have tremendous relevance today.
As this book was being written, company after company in
North America and Europe was under siege from investors,
shareholders, and securities regulators with issues ranging
from possible irregularities to downright fraud in the
reporting of their financial results.   The list is long and
familiar to most readers, including: Enron, Adelphia,
Worldcom, AOL Time Warner, Ahold, and others.   Not to
suggest that traditional budgeting processes are the primary
cause, but certainly the ease by which top management can
simply set or change a budget to meet its own and/or the
investment community's objectives are well known.   Once
these unrealistic changes are in place, then organizations feel

---

[6] Bossidy, L. and R. Charan. 2002. *Execution: The Discipline of Getting
Things Done*. New York, NY: Random House Inc., 228-229.

committed to deliver on those targets, lest their share prices be negatively affected. This pressure to deliver the results driven from budgets is one of the causal links behind the recent flood of accounting improprieties.

The research that underpins this book shows that many of the challenges with traditional budget processes are generic and endemic. These challenges or issues occur across all industries and types of organizations and can be grouped into three major categories:

- Issues with preparing the budget,

- Issues of efficiency and effectiveness, and

- Issues with people.

While the issues are categorized and separated to simplify the discussion, in reality they are inter-twined. Their interactive effect is the cause of much of the dissatisfaction with the budget process and hence its results.

1.2.1 Issues with Preparing the Budget

DILBERT reprinted by permission of United Feature Syndicate, Inc.

1. *The budget is all too frequently based on an optimistic sales or pessimistic funding forecast.*   In the private sector, management generally biases revenue forecasts upwards to show growth and vitality; in the public sector, the reverse is usually true in order to demonstrate the need for a larger budget to meet the increasing workload.

2. *The budget is usually based on an extrapolation of prior periods' revenues and expenses.*   While true in many functions, this issue is particularly true in the traditional "overhead" or support ones, such as the sales, general, and administration functions.

3. *The process is shrouded in secrecy.*   Because the budget deals with payroll information and plans for future changes in compensation, along with other sensitive matters such as customer and supplier contracts, the sharing of information during the budgeting process is often limited.

4. *The process suffers from a lack of ownership.*   Many people feel that they are alienated from the budget process and that they are feeding a process they don't understand.   Conversely, many others who participate at the fringes of the process feel little or no ownership for their work and care nothing about its success.

5. *The budget is often prepared at the last minute.* With the exception of the financial units, the budget process is rarely a top priority in anyone's mind until it is about to be worked on.

1.2.2 Issues of Effectiveness and Efficiency

DILBERT reprinted by permission of United Feature Syndicate, Inc.

6. *The budgeting cycle is too long.* In most organizations, the typical annual budget cycle starts several months before the new fiscal period begins, but often continues into the new period!

7. *The process requires too many iterations.* As management attempts to bring the proposed budgets – all of which are "gamed" to the advantage of each submitting unit - closer to achieving the unstated operational and financial targets, the number of iterations grows, the cycle time increases, and frustration rises.

8. *The process is too fragmented.* In many large organizations, the impact that some units, particularly

service operations, have on other units' performance and cost is poorly understood.

9. *Contingency plans are not built into the budget.* Few, if any, budgets provide for the extra resources to address unknown changes in the business environment, such as a competitor entering a particular sales region or a shift in the regulatory environment.

10. *The approved budget is often not current enough.* When the environment changes quickly, as is the case in so many industries and organizations today, a long budget cycle will often generate obsolete budgets.

11. *Potential capacity problems are not addressed.* While management knows that actual volumes are inevitably going to be above or below the budget forecast, most do not have a system in place that can measure the impact on resources.

12. *The process does not include a review of prior period budget assumptions.* Much time goes into discussing, analyzing, and reacting to variances from the budget, but there is no formal review of the prior budget's assumptions and the impact of incorrect or inaccurate assumptions on actual results.

1.2.3 Issues with People

DILBERT reprinted by permission of United Feature Syndicate, Inc.

13. *The process loses credibility due to gaming.* The entire planning and/or budgeting process loses credibility when individuals are required to submit data they know is wrong or will be changed, simply to feed the process. The traditional budget process almost always includes extensive gaming, results manipulation, and occasionally outright lies.

14. *Budgeting is seen as a one-time event.* In most organizations, the budget process is an annual event, and is usually seen in precisely that light: "It's budget

time again." As a result, very little thought goes into the process itself or how to improve it.

15. *The process is played on an uneven field.* Less experienced employees do not know the elements that influence decisions, the key decision-makers, or the factors deemed most important to the organization, and thus may not be able to obtain a fair share of resources for their unit.

16. *The process suffers from a lack of communication.* The final budget process is rarely communicated to lower levels and individuals who participate are often unsure of the final outcome. Even those keenly interested in the budget process are kept uninformed.

17. *The process is not completed consistently year to year.* The budget process is not very well maintained or controlled by most organizations, and as a result is not understood. In many cases, documentation of the prior period's process is not available.

18. *The planning process has many unpublished expectations.* Quite often management has very strong implicit expectations about what the final budget should be, generated by their own experience, forecasts given to the investment community, internal performance targets, compensation plans, or political reasons. Yet these expectations are not conveyed to line managers

other than through seemingly arbitrary changes to budget requests or revenue projections.

19. *Employees do not buy into a process they do not understand.* Whether it is the budget process or any other, employees rarely support or put a solid effort into a process they do not understand or believe in.

20. *The process places uneven requirements on budget participants.* The amount of work, gaming, and stress that goes into the preparation of the annual budget varies greatly between functions and within each function.

In summary, both the traditional budget process and the results of that process are flawed and may add little value to the organization. Many of these challenges can be overcome by following a more integrative, systematic budgeting approach.

1.3 THE CAM-I ABPB CLOSED-LOOP MODEL

This book proposes a new planning and budgeting framework, the CAM-I ABPB Closed-Loop Model, summarized in Figure 1.1. The Closed-Loop Model is the calculation engine that lies at the heart of the broader ABPB Process.

Figure 1.1: The CAM-I ABPB Closed-Loop Model

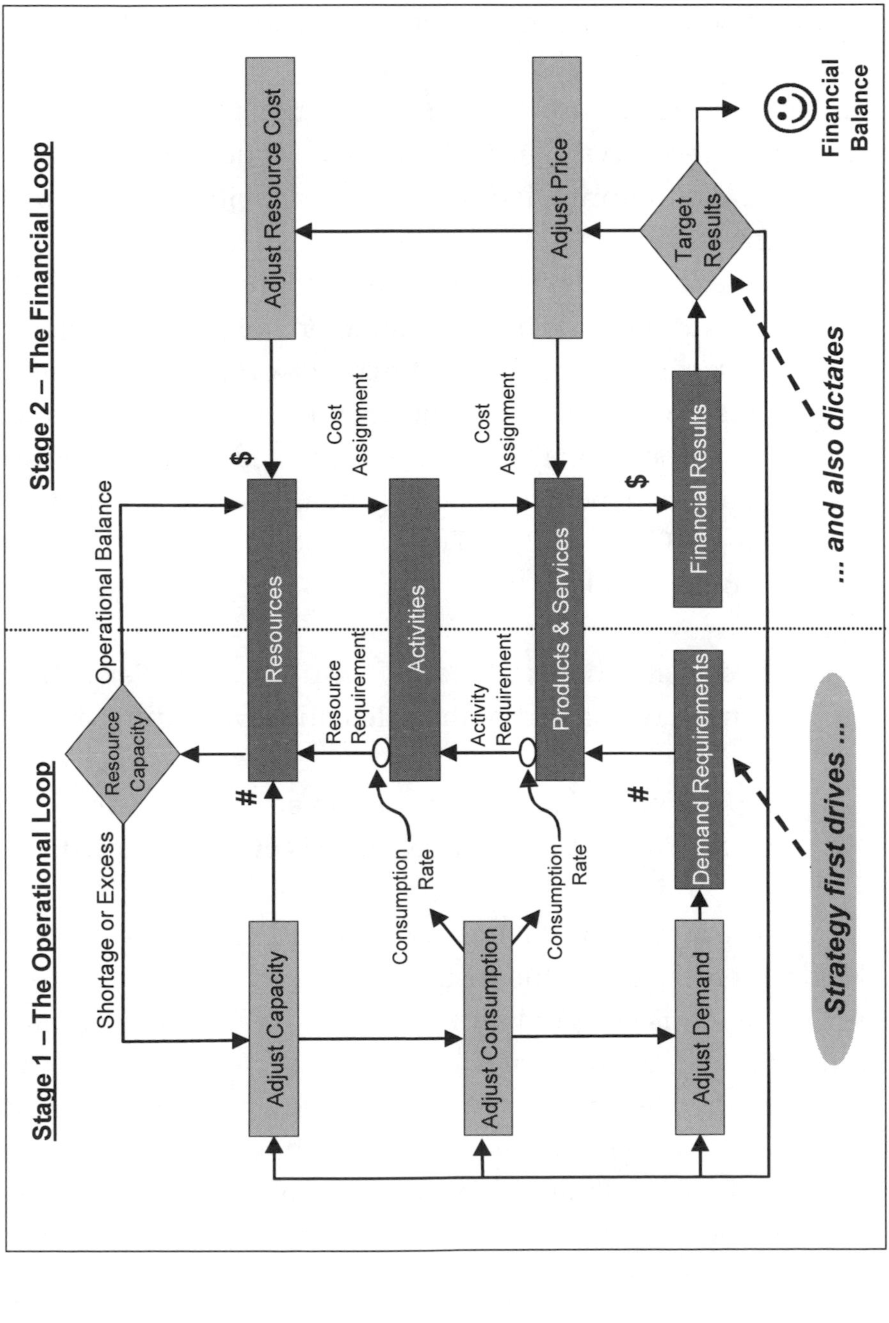

As with all planning and budgeting approaches, the Closed-Loop Model begins with the organization's strategy. Strategy guides the level of demand for products and services, which in turn generates demands for activities and ultimately resources. The Closed-Loop Model explicitly uses activity-based information to generate activity and resource requirements.

The next step is to compare resource demand with resource supply. The organization explicitly adjusts resource capacity, resource and activity consumption rates, or product demand forecasts until an operational balance is achieved. Operational balance is achieved when resource supply and demand are roughly equal (a full definition is provided in Chapter 2). Two additional features of the Closed-Loop Model are that:

1. Resource demand and supply are explicitly considered as part of the calculation procedure, and

2. Operational balance is achieved before financial budgeting and financial balance is even attempted.

Once operational balance is achieved, the Closed-Loop Model then calculates the costs of resources, links those costs with the costs of activities, the costs of products, and ultimately with projected financial performance. The organization then uses the projected financial numbers to investigate financial balance and feasibility. If these results do not satisfy the financial targets, which are typically set as part of the organization's strategy or established as key planning assumptions, then the organization can seek to adjust unit resource costs and/or unit prices to achieve financial balance, and/or seek to influence the operational plan.

In total, the organization has three distinct levers to achieve operational balance and two additional levers to achieve financial balance, and therefore has five levers to achieve both:

1. Quantity and/or mix of product demands,

2. Resource and activity consumption rates,

3. Resource capacity,

4. Unit resource costs, and

5. Unit prices for products and services.

Unlike traditional budgeting approaches, the Closed-Loop Model considers all possible methods to achieve financial balance and an acceptable budget.

1.4 THE ISSUES OVERCOME AND NOT OVERCOME WITH THE CLOSED-LOOP MODEL

The Closed-Loop Model can help solve or alleviate many of the issues and challenges facing traditional budgeting processes. However, it is not a panacea for all of the flaws in most budgeting processes. Table 1.2 identifies the specific issues that the Closed-Loop Model resolves or minimizes, as well as those that it does not adequately address.

The following paragraphs discuss how the Closed-Loop Model helps resolve many of the challenges with traditional budgeting processes (references are to those issues noted in Table 1.2).

Issue 1. *The budget is all too frequently based on an optimistic sales or pessimistic funding forecast.* If an overly optimistic sales forecast is introduced into an ABPB Process, the resulting resource requirements will cause executives and operating managers to question both the resource requirements and the capabilities of existing processes to deliver against the forecast.

Issue 2. *The budget is usually based on an extrapolation of prior periods' revenues and expenses.* In contrast, the Closed-Loop   Model   uses   activity-based   logic, consumption rates, and resource capacities to determine resource requirements and costs.   Further, the Closed-Loop Model can be updated to contain all of the latest changes to products and processes, as well as costs.

Issue 3. *The process is shrouded in secrecy.* In addition to staff having access to regular accounting and financial data, all operating managers should be involved in the preparation of the activity-based budget.   Because activity-based data drills down to a lower level of the organization than the traditional budget, more people can be involved in planning and budgeting.

Table 1.2: The Issues Overcome and Not Overcome by the Closed-Loop Model

ISSUES	OVERCOME
Preparing the Budget	
1. Optimistic sales forecast	Yes
2. Extrapolating prior periods' numbers	Yes
3. Shrouded in secrecy	Yes
4. Lack of ownership	Yes
5. Done at the last minute	No
Effectiveness and Efficiency	
6. Too long a cycle	Yes
7. Too many iterations	Yes
8. Too fragmented a process	Yes
9. Contingencies not included	Not explicitly
10. Budget not current enough	Yes
11. Capacity problems not addressed	Yes
12. No review of prior periods' budget assumptions	No
People	
13. Gaming reduces credibility	Yes
14. Viewed as one-time event	Yes
15. Uneven knowledge of process	Not fully
16. Lack of communication	Yes
17. Lack of consistency between periods	Yes
18. Many unpublished expectations	Not fully
19. Lack of employee buy-in	Yes
20. Uneven requirements on participants	No

Issue 4. *The process suffers from a lack of ownership.* As the mystery of the budgeting process becomes linked to data from the regular operations and accounting systems, ownership and credibility improve. Estimated costs are based on activity history and actual operating performance, since connecting the budget with hard data leaves less room for disagreement. As employees feel more confident in their ability to navigate the system, they gain confidence in the process and as a result, gaming diminishes. As the budget process becomes clearer to those involved in it, its use as a management tool increases.

Issues 6 and 7. *The budgeting cycle is too long and requires too many iterations.* These two issues are inextricably linked because the number of iterations invariably increases the length of the whole cycle. Over time, agreement will increase on the approximate cost of processes and activities and what drives cost behavior. Disagreements can be addressed more rapidly because they can be resolved by looking at past activity and operational performance. The integrated nature of ABPB allows faster and more comprehensive analyses.

Issue 8. *The process is too fragmented.* Using common activity-based information across the operating and accounting systems allows the entire organization to use the same information in the budget process. Thus, a single set of assumptions drives strategy, operating parameters, and financial parameters. These assumptions permit operational balance to be measured on the same basis as financial balance and for performance to be measured on that same basis.

Issue 10. *The approved budget is often not current enough.* The Closed-Loop Model permits faster updates than traditional approaches, thus allowing for more frequent updates, each reflecting current knowledge of business conditions.

Issue 11. *Potential capacity problems are not addressed.* A unique feature of the Closed-Loop Model is its explicit consideration of capacity, which, in turn, forces the explicit recognition of capacity in the development of operating and financial plans. As such, the Closed-Loop Model allows management to respond to changes in demand by addressing resource allocation and/or absolute levels of capacity.

Issues 13 and 19. *The process loses credibility due to gaming and is not bought into.* Employees game the system, in part, because they know that any misleading information they submit will not be caught. With Activity-Based Planning and Budgeting, causal relationships are identified and quantified. This increase in the transparency of the process reduces the ability of managers to game the system. As users then become more confident in the process itself, the credibility of the process will improve.

Issue 14. *The budget is seen as a one-time event.* The ABPB Process is designed to operate throughout the year, regularly updating management by analyzing actual results and refining expectations for the future, which can be reflected in future iterations of the model.

Issue 16. *The process suffers from a lack of communication.* The final product of the budgeting process can easily be updated because much of the information is automated through the operating and accounting systems. Because much of the data is at a more granular activity level, providing units with the final budget numbers should be easier.

Issue 17. *The process is not completed consistently period-to-period.* A model based explicitly on the business unit's operating parameters and demand-activity-resource linkages is inherently more consistent period-to-period. These relationships tend to be fairly stable over the time horizon of a budget and any changes to activities and resources can be readily understood.

The ABPB Process is a significantly improved planning and budgeting tool, but may not reduce the number of iterations in the budgeting process. Although it may take fewer iterations to achieve each operationally and financially balanced budget, management may use the planning and budgeting process to zero in on and improve business planning. This may increase the total number of iterations.

What is clear however is that each iteration will be of substantially greater value than was previously the case.

An approach that explicitly links operational performance with financial results forces an organization's budget to more realistically reflect its capabilities. The Closed-Loop Model will make it apparent that the achievement of overly-optimistic revenue and/or growth targets or cost reductions simply may not be doable given the existing operating conditions. Management will have to publicly over-ride the budgeting system in order to generate budgets with overly generous assumptions. Therefore, the use of a rigorous approach, such as ABPB, is a step forward in improving the integrity of organizational planning and budgeting and supports improvements in the integrity of financial reporting in general.

1.5 THE NECESSARY KNOWLEDGE BASE

While the Closed-Loop Model initially appears to be complex, there are only two necessary precursors: activity-based analysis and process analysis. Figure 1.3 illustrates the evolution toward ABPB.

The first precursor is activity-based analysis, which leads to the development of relationships and measures that are important in the understanding of the activities and supporting resources. The second precursor is process analysis, which allows a unit to understand the set of activities that contribute to producing its outputs, be they products or services. An existing Activity-Based Cost Management (ABCM) system can be the source for much of

Figure 1.3: The Evolution of Activity-Based Planning and Budgeting

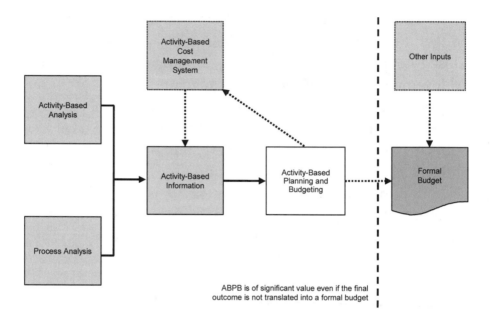

ABPB is of significant value even if the final
outcome is not translated into a formal budget

this information.

Combining process and activity-based analyses leads to activity-based information, including activity and resource consumption rates and resource capacity details.   This activity-based information can then be combined with volume forecasts to predict the resources required in a future period. This is called Activity-Based Planning. The resource requirements from this plan can then be costed to form the Activity-Based Budget.

When appropriate, the Activity-Based Budget figures can be used along with other non activity-based calculations in the development of the formal budget. A formal budget is defined as a document with the proper executive approval(s) that includes sufficient detail of organization resources, including labor, non-labor, and statement of work forecasts, to represent an organization's strategic and operational plan for the upcoming business period. In many organizations, a formal budget is a required document for management control and measurement purposes.

Formal budgets are still most commonly formulated on an annual basis, whereas Activity-Based Planning and Budgeting can be conducted on a more frequent or as required basis.

Although Activity-Based Planning and Budgeting will usually result in a formal budget, there is significant value to the Closed-Loop Model even if the results are not explicitly reported in the formal budget. The Closed-Loop Model ensures that the organization's plans are feasible and based upon the organization's overall strategy. In addition, the delineation of the organization's activities, processes, and resources provides useful information for both control and improvement.

Figure 1.3 illustrates an important additional point. Although it would aid in developing the model, an ABCM system does not *have* to be in place in order to use Activity-Based Planning and Budgeting.[7] Nevertheless, having an ABCM process or system in place will be of major benefit to

---

[7] In some organizations, Activity-Based Planning and Budgeting has preceded and led to the development of Activity-Based Cost Management (Sanders 1995).

organizations seeking to implement ABPB. The two approaches share key building blocks: demand items (products and services), activities, and resources. They follow comparable logic, although it must be emphasized that ABPB is not ABC in reverse, as will be explained further in Chapter 3. Thus, while perhaps not a pre-requisite to implementing ABPB, having an ABCM process in place – and more importantly, having an activity-based mindset – will greatly simplify and assist in the implementation of ABPB.

The next section turns to an overview of the content and structure of the book.

1.6 AN OVERVIEW

CAM-I formed the ABPB Interest Group in response to the growing concerns of the private and public sectors with respect to budgets and budgeting processes. The Group consists of managers of budgeting processes, consultants to enterprises developing and using budgets, planning and budgeting software developers, and academics. All were dismayed by the abysmal state of budgeting as they keenly felt many of the problems with current budget practice. The Group's mission was to assess whether the budgeting process could be improved by incorporating Activity-Based Cost Management concepts into the planning and budgeting arena, and if so, how.

In its early stages, the Group surveyed the available literature on Activity-Based Planning and Budgeting. The results of this search are captured in the Bibliography.

The Group's first major output was to develop a calculation tool that incorporates activity-based logic and information. The CAM-I ABPB Closed-Loop Model, shown in Figure 1.1, was the result. Chapter 2 presents the algorithm in detail, while Chapter 3 provides a service organization example. Chapter 4 shows how the Closed-Loop Model can be extended to government cost recovery settings, government program settings, and shared service environments.

Once the Group finished developing the Closed-Loop Model, it immediately turned to the challenge of how to implement and sustain it in an organization. In moving through the initial implementation of a Closed-Loop Model in a single business unit to having an ongoing enterprise-wide Activity-Based Planning and Budgeting Process, an organization will follow a commonly used program management structure:

- Initial or pilot implementation of a Closed-Loop Model, managed as an ABPB Implementation Project,

- Expansion of the Closed-Loop Model to new areas of the organization, each implementation conducted as a project and all projects collectively managed in the ABPB Implementation Program, and

- Ultimately maintaining and updating each Closed-Loop Model, and the organization's network of Closed-Loop Models, through an easily sustainable ABPB Process.   As each unit completes its implementation, the ABPB Process will spread throughout the organization.

Part 2 of this book follows this project management structure. The first four chapters deal with a single implementation of a Closed-Loop Model. Chapter 5 describes the project management approach that guides each implementation of a Closed-Loop Model, and the transition towards the ABPB Implementation Program. Chapter 6 explicitly addresses the issue of ABPB Project Management at the tactical level and offers a "Ten Step" guide for orchestrating the Initiating and Planning phases of each Project. Chapter 7 takes the reader from the tactical to the operational level, addressing issues such as understanding the planning horizon, the Closed-Loop Model building blocks, collecting the necessary data, and linking it all together. Chapter 8 shows how to use the new, more sophisticated budget to analyze actual to plan deviations.

Chapter 9 adds in the supporting elements that turn the calculation engine, the Closed-Loop Model, into a self-sustaining business process, the ABPB Process, that is understood and accepted by the entire organization.
This sequence of chapters 5 through 9 provides the reader with the necessary background and expertise to successfully initiate, plan, execute, and control the ABPB Implementation Program. At the end of the Program, the organization will have embedded the ABPB Process, shown in Figure 1.4, which consists of all of the necessary elements needed to sustain all of its' Closed-Loop Models.

Figure 1.4: The CAM-I ABPB Process

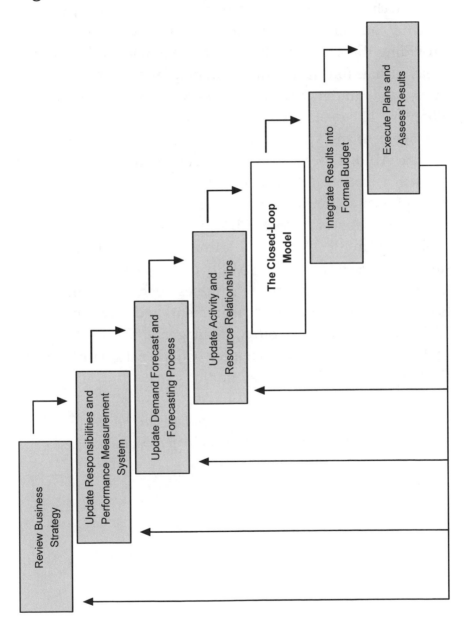

Two additional chapters in Part 2 provide support with more technical details. Chapter 10 delves deeper into specific building blocks of the Closed-Loop Model, providing the reader with advanced knowledge in selected areas such as forecasting demand, determining consumption rates, and understanding complex activity interactions. Chapter 11 deals with the issues relating to data management and systems architecture.

The ABPB Process is a management tool and does not exist in isolation. Part 3 of this book examines how the ABPB Process interfaces with other management processes. Chapter 12 shows how ABPB can co-exist with traditional budgeting in developing a formal budget. Chapter 13 demonstrates how to link ABPB concepts with other key performance management techniques such as the Balanced Scorecard, Performance Measurement and Benchmarking, Risk Management, Resource Management, and Capacity Optimization. The final chapter, Chapter 14, summarizes the book and the Group's key findings.

Now that the book's structure has been laid out, the next chapter begins by describing the Closed-Loop Model in detail.

2 CHAPTER

Details of the ABPB Closed-Loop Model

2.1 AN OVERVIEW

The CAM-I ABPB Closed-Loop Model is a recommended approach for developing an operationally feasible and financially acceptable budget that is linked to the overall strategy of the organization. It is designed for a specific time period, but not necessarily an annual time period. Figure 2.1 provides an overview of the broad stages in the Closed-Loop Model.

The Closed-Loop Model contains two stages. The trigger for the Closed-Loop Model is the establishment or review of the organization's strategy (or a periodic decision to review its operations). The first stage uses the organization's strategy to develop an operational plan for a specific time period. Based on the strategy and the projected demands for the organization, the operational plan must strike a balance between the quantity of resources needed to fulfill the demands and the available capacity of each such resource; this state is referred to as "Operational Balance".

Operational balance is defined as: *providing sufficient*

Figure 2.1: Overview of the CAM-I ABPB Closed-Loop Model

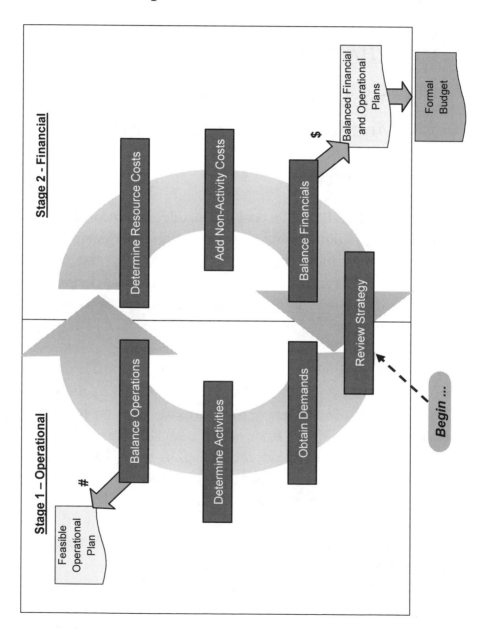

individual and aggregate resource capacity to meet each and all demands placed on the organization with an acceptable level of unused capacity. Unused capacity may be considered in a positive sense as reserve or buffer capacity, or in a negative sense as excess capacity.

The first stage of the Closed-Loop Model results in a viable operational plan. A plan is not operationally balanced if the available capacity is less than the quantity of resource that is required or demanded. The most important aspect of operational balance is that it must be achieved in purely non-financial terms (e.g., machine hours required must balance with the machine hours of available capacity).

The second stage of the Closed-Loop Model is the development of a financial plan, which is based on the operational plan. The financial plan should ultimately achieve the required financial balance.

Financial balance is defined as: *generating a financial plan and/or budget that uses the quantities and rates defined in the operational plan to deliver the required financial results (e.g., EVA, return on sales, absolute profitability).*

A plan is not financially balanced if the financial results predicted by the Closed-Loop Model fail to meet the pre-determined targets as set out in the review of strategy.

While the concepts are straightforward, performing the necessary calculations is fairly intricate. Figure 2.2 provides the additional detail needed to generate the predicted results.

The sections that follow explain more fully the detailed steps within each stage.

Figure 2.2: The CAM-I ABPB Closed-Loop Model

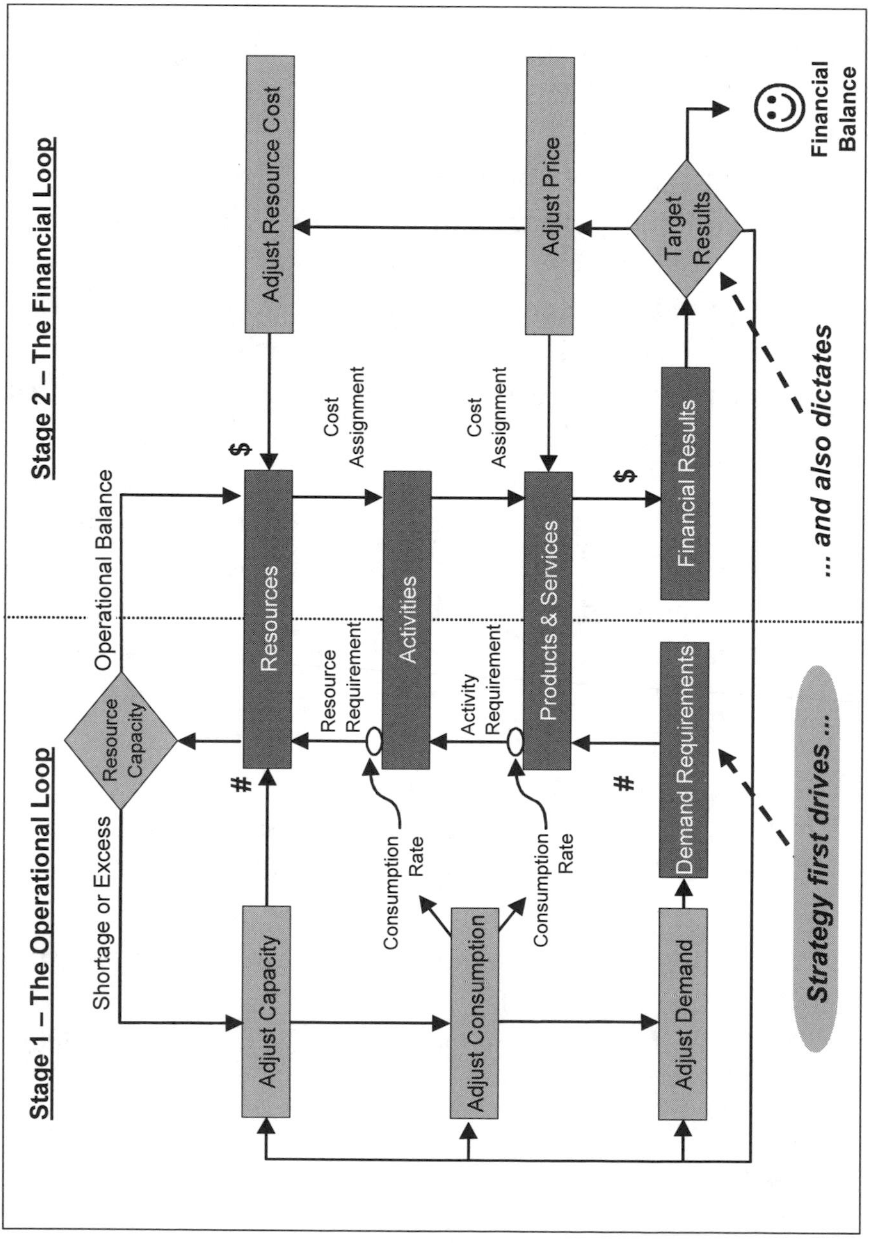

Stage 2 – The Financial Loop

Stage 1 – The Operational Loop

Adjust Resource Cost

Adjust Price

Target Results

Financial Balance

Cost Assignment

Cost Assignment

Operational Balance

$

$

Resources

Activities

Products & Services

Financial Results

... and also dictates

Resource Capacity

Shortage or Excess

#

Resource Requirement

Activity Requirement

#

Demand Requirements

Consumption Rate

Consumption Rate

Adjust Capacity

Adjust Consumption

Adjust Demand

Strategy first drives ...

2.2 STAGE 1: ACHIEVING OPERATIONAL BALANCE

Stage one of the Closed-Loop Model consists of three steps:

Step 1. Set quantitative demands,

Step 2. Determine resource requirements, and

Step 3. Balance resource requirements with resource
    supply.

2.2.1 Step 1: Set Quantitative Demands

Using the organization's strategy, the quantity of demand in the upcoming period is estimated for each product or service.   This estimation is done purely in quantitative terms, such as number of units, tons, accounts, customers, shipments, service levels, and so on, and must be completed for each distinct product or service.   This is shown in Figure 2.3.[8]

In setting demands, offerings that are similar but that have different levels of service must be defined as two or more products or services. For example, a help desk staffed on a 7x24 basis (i.e. 7 days at 24 hours per day) is a distinct service from a help desk that performs identical activities but staffed on a 5x24 basis.

---

[8] In most cases, the estimation of quantity is intimately linked with the selling or transfer price, i.e. revenue. Therefore, it is likely that unit price estimates are available at the same time, but these will only be used in Stage 2.

Figure 2.3: Setting Quantitative Demands

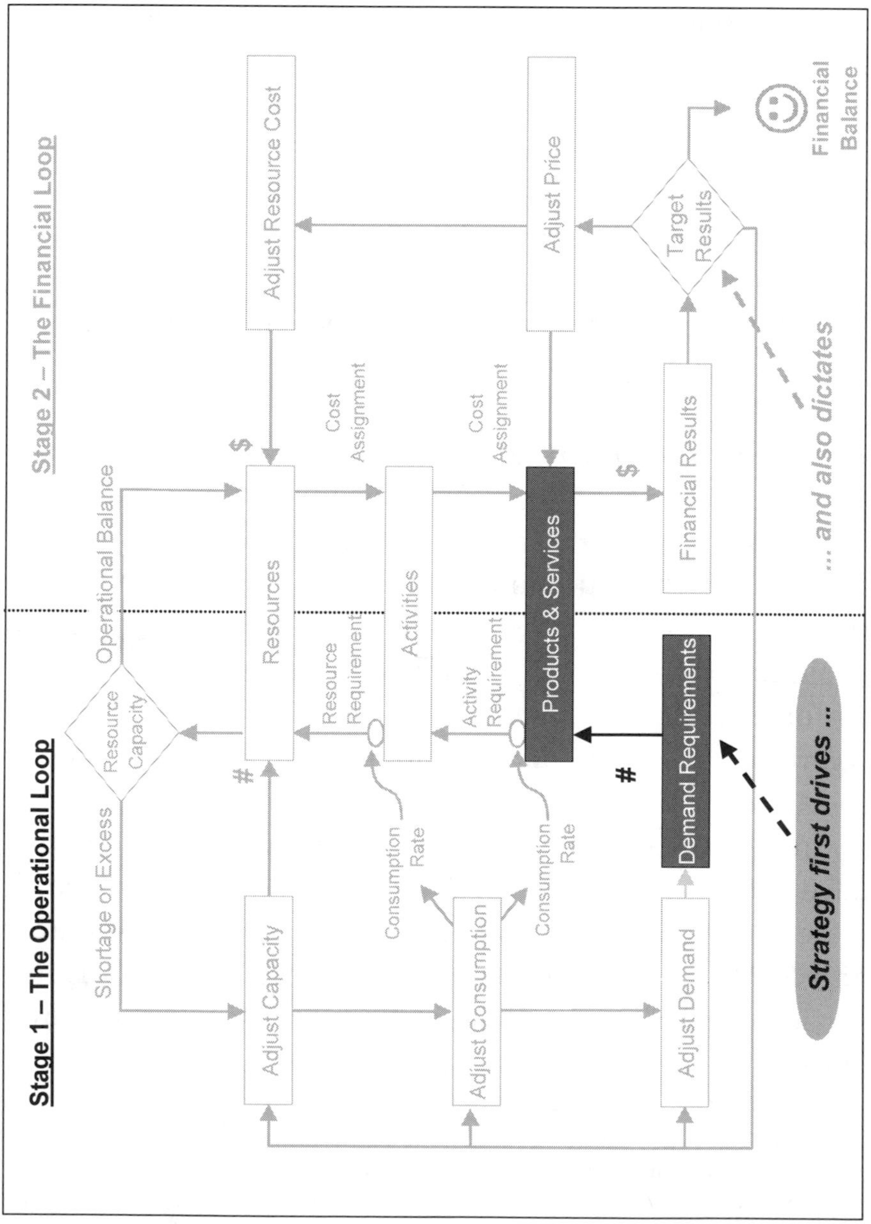

2.2.2 Step 2: Determine Resource Requirements

Step two in the Closed-Loop Model consists of two distinct actions.

First, the quantity of demand is converted into activity requirements, expressed in operational terms, using activity consumption rates. Activity consumption rates are defined as: *the number of occurrences of an activity required to generate a single unit of output.* Activity consumption rates include things such the number of calls per marketing campaign or the number of inspections per batch. The activity consumption rate defines the volume of work required to generate a unit of output, but it does not consider who or what will do the work.

Second, the activity requirements are converted into individual resource requirements, using resource consumption rates. Resource consumption rates are defined as: *the quantity of each resource required to undertake a single occurrence of an activity.* Resource consumption rates include things such as the number of minutes per call, the number of minutes per inspection, or cubic footage of inventory by product. Thus, the resource consumption rate defines the quantity of each resource required to complete one unit of activity.

Consumption rates must be known or approximated to develop an estimate of activity and resource requirements. Typically, consumption rates are drawn from existing operational data, including activity-based information, but the rates may be modified to accommodate known or planned changes for the specific period of the budget.

After completing these actions, an organization will have
an estimate of the required quantity of each resource,
expressed in the unit of measure of each resource, as shown
in Figure 2.4.   For example, personnel requirements are
typically measured in full-time equivalents (FTEs) or hours
by   position,   equipment   in   machine   hours,
telecommunications in bandwidth metrics, and space in
square footage. Quantifying resources at this level cannot be
done with traditional budgeting tools or mechanisms,
because those methods do not use consumption rates in a
systematic manner, if at all.

2.2.3 Step 3: Balance Resource Requirements with Resource Supply

The most critical aspect of the Closed-Loop Model is
establishing operational balance by matching resource
requirements with resource capacity in a given time period.
The Closed-Loop Model allows organizations to match
resource supply with an estimate of future resource
requirements.   The Closed-Loop Model also works in
situations where the timeframe of resource supply is
different from the timeframe of the budget. For example, an
airline might lease an airplane for 10 years but budget its use
on an annual basis.   The Closed-Loop Model explicitly
allows organizations to "set aside" a share of capacity as
"Idle Marketable" as part of the balancing process (see
Chapter 8 for details).

Figure 2.4: Determining Resource Requirements

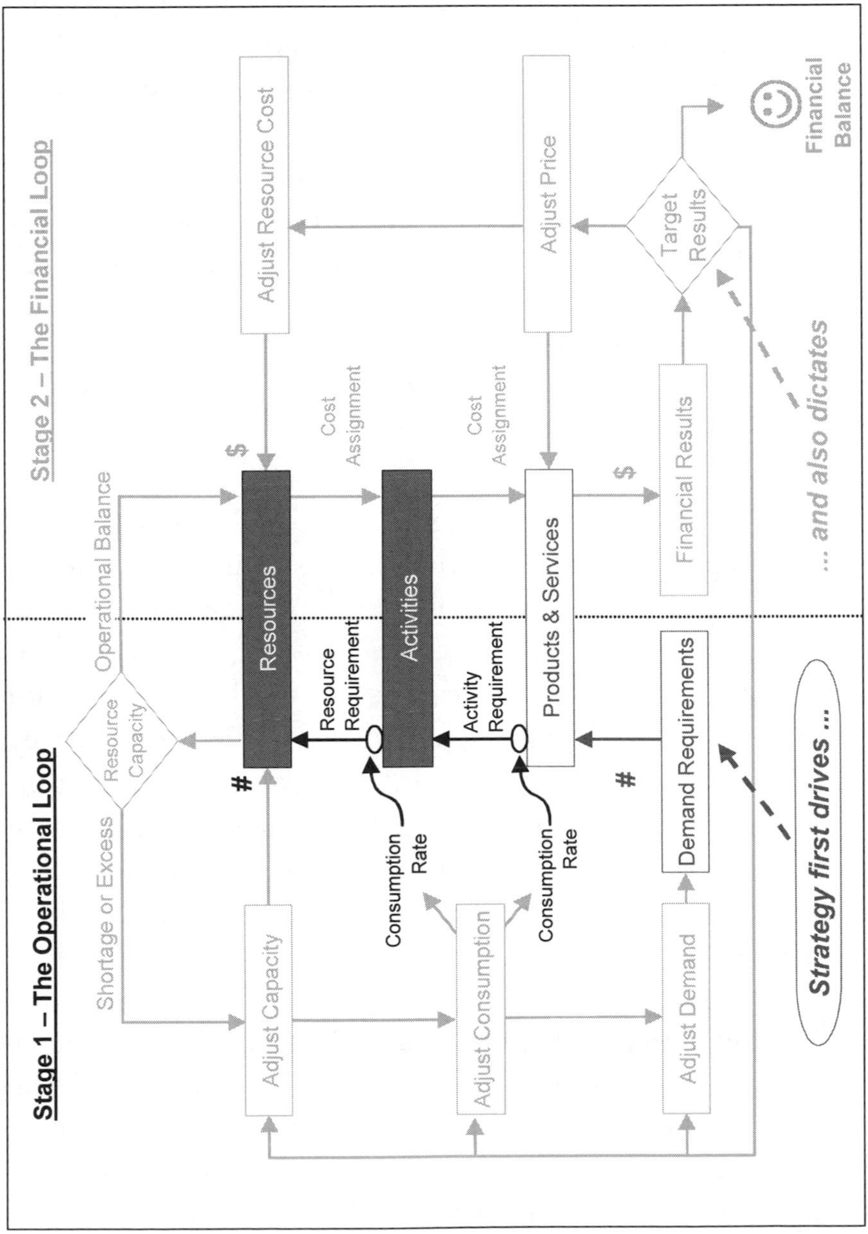

The practical difficulty in comparing resources supplied and resources required occurs when the unit of measure used for the supply of a resource differs from the unit of measure in which the resource is used.   Consider these examples:

- Requirements for people are often expressed in hours, whereas people are generally acquired in FTEs,

- Equipment requirements may be expressed in machine hours, whereas they are purchased as whole machines, and

- Office space requirements are usually expressed in square feet but acquired or leased in larger blocks, such as whole or partial floors.

Management must determine a single measure for supply, demand, and capacity for each resource by translating expressions of units into a common denominator.

Once a capacity measure is determined, management compares each resource's supply with its corresponding requirement.   This comparison results in one of three situations:

1. **Too much capacity**: Demand requirements can be met, but there will be idle or excess capacity, causing a higher than optimal cost structure.   Too much capacity may be operationally feasible but is only operationally balanced if the amount of excess

capacity is necessary as a buffer. If this is the case, the situation needs to be analyzed to see if it meets financial balance.

2. **Too little capacity**: Demand requirements cannot be met because there is a shortage of resources. This situation is not operationally feasible and therefore cannot be operationally balanced.[9]

3. **Exact balance of capacity and demand**: This situation is operationally feasible and, by definition, in operational balance. The situation needs to be analyzed to see if it meets financial balance.

Armed with the knowledge of any imbalances, management must assess capacity by determining whether or not:

- A surplus or shortage of resources is large enough to justify action or if it should just be accepted. For example, a small shortfall might be met with acceptable amounts of overtime, the use of management staff, or contractors. Conversely, a small amount of idle capacity might be appropriate to

---

[9] The Closed-Loop Model is a calculation algorithm. As such, it will treat a situation where resources required exceed resources supplied as infeasible, and therefore the organization could theoretically not meet its demand requirements. In extreme cases this may be true. However, in many cases, the use of overtime, temporary labor, or extremely high machine utilization – especially in short time periods – may be employed to meet demand. This case is, in effect, a new plan with greater capacity and higher cost.

provide a capacity buffer, ensure that service levels meet or exceed requirements, or to permit meeting unexpected demand.

- The surplus or shortage is expected to last for a long time. Shortages that continue for a long period can cause excessive costs for overtime or decreased performance or service levels. In a surplus situation, the justification for holding buffer capacity "just in case" might become strained if that capacity is never used.

- The capacity cannot be changed in the time horizon being addressed, given prevailing economic conditions. For example, in a tight labor market, acquiring additional labor resources might be both difficult and more costly than planned. Similarly, in the power generation industry, the lead time required to add capacity is generally measured in years (or in some jurisdictions, in decades) due to the lengthy regulatory, capital acquisition, and construction times required. Thus, adding capacity in the short run may be very difficult.[10]

---

[10] This is especially true at the macro or industry level, although somewhat less so at the organization level. For example, an individual power distributor in need of capacity is often able to purchase power from other suppliers whose peak demand patterns are different. But the industry as a whole has an absolute capacity limit that cannot be safely exceeded.

With a capacity assessment in hand, there are three distinct ways that the organization can achieve operational balance, as shown in Figure 2.5:

1. *Adjust capacity or improve the usage of resources.* A resource surplus can be resolved by eliminating excess capacity or by finding alternative means to consume available resources. Conversely, a resource shortage can be addressed by adding capacity internally through resource acquisition or externally by outsourcing. With operational balance, the demand requirements can be met, and there is either no excess capacity or an acceptable quantity of idle or buffer capacity.

2. *Adjust the activity and/or resource consumption rates to resolve, or at least to reduce, the magnitude of the problem.* Management usually seeks to implement any available economic efficiency and effectiveness opportunity. For example, process changes might be made to reduce resource requirements or perhaps to increase quality or service levels, and thus consume otherwise excess resource capacity. It may seem unusual to consider the possibility of increasing a consumption rate in order to consume excess capacity, but if demand can't be increased and resources are fixed at a certain level, perhaps increasing service quality without adding resources may create a competitive advantage for the organization.

Figure 2.5: Obtaining Operational Balance

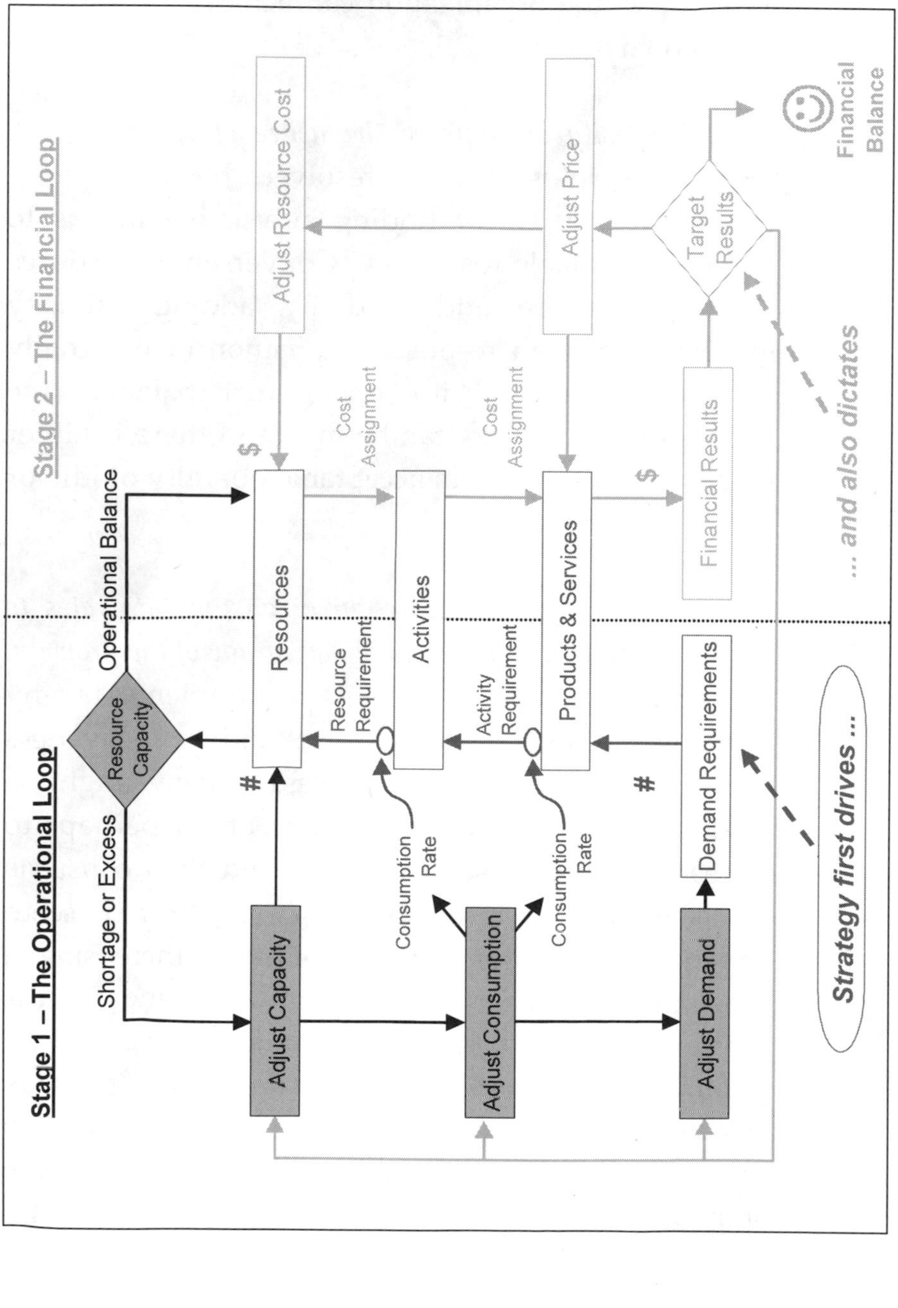

3. *Change the absolute mix of products/services demanded.* A well planned product change may either absorb the excess or reduce the shortage of resources without affecting the organization's overall strategy.

While these three options are presented sequentially, this is done solely for illustrative purposes and is not meant to recommend any order.   The optimal sequence would depend upon the specific business environment.

As was shown in Figure 2.5, the interplay of the quantities of demand, consumption rates, and resource supply is repeated until operational balance is reached. Achieving operational balance means that the organization as a whole, and each of its units, is able to meet the expected demand with an acceptable quantity of resources. After the decision on resource supply is made, the Closed-Loop Model moves to the next stage, achieving financial balance.

2.3 STAGE 2: ACHIEVING FINANCIAL BALANCE

Much like the process of achieving operational balance, achieving financial balance is an iterative process of assessing alternatives and results. The goal of this stage of the Closed-Loop Model is to predict financial results based on the demand quantities used in the operational plan and the quantity of resources required.   Financial balance is reached when the predicted results match the required targets set by management. For example, the organization might set 12% return on sales as the profitability target for the period. Another, more sophisticated, example is that the organization may set an 8% return on capital target. This measure of financial balance incorporates the incremental costs of expanding capacity and reflects the idea that all organizations have limited financial resources. Financial balance is reached only when the cost of resources, combined with the quantity of each product demanded and its unit price, results in meeting the targets.

Continuing from the three steps of Stage 1, achieving financial balance consists of four steps:

Step 4. Determine resource costs and derive financial results,

Step 5. Add non-activity-based costs to obtain the total financial results,

Step 6. Balance financial results with financial targets, and

Step 7. Create a formal budget.

2.3.1 Step 4: Determine Resource Costs and Derive Financial Results

To determine resource costs, two elements are required: the unit cost of each resource required and the quantity of each resource as determined from the operational plan. The total cost for each resource can be calculated by multiplying the unit requirement by the appropriate unit price, although this calculation can involve more complex formulae or weighting.   Total resource cost is determined simply by adding up the individual cost of each resource.[11]   This is shown in the arrows coming down from "Operational Balance" through to "Financial Results" in Figure 2.6.

The financial elements needed to complete this step are the:

- Unit cost of resources, such as the hourly wage or annual salary, and

- Revenue (price) per unit of demand.

The cost of each resource is assigned to the resource, and using the relationship between each resource and each activity, these costs can be assigned to the activities requiring or consuming that resource.   These activity costs are then assigned to products to derive product and service costs.

2.3.2 Step 5: Add Non-Activity-Based Costs to Obtain Total Financial Results

Certain organizational costs may not have a direct or tangible correlation with activity volume and, therefore, are

---

[11] When determining resource costs, care must be taken to include only those costs that vary with the usage or existence of the resource. For example, in the case of vehicle costs, one would include the period operating and licensing costs of each type of vehicle, along with the corresponding depreciation charge, but the capital cost would be excluded.

Figure 2.6: Determining Resource Costs and Calculating Financial Results

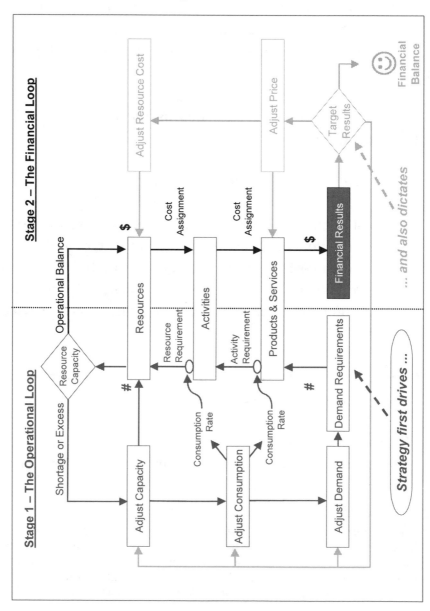

better handled through a more traditional budgeting approach than the Closed-Loop Model. These types of costs are sometimes referred to as "business sustaining" costs. Examples of business sustaining costs are directors' fees, certain building leases, Securities and Exchange Commission filing fees, etc. Ultimately, all costs (activity-based and non-activity-based) that apply to the organization must be considered to generate a financial plan, as shown in Figure 2.7.

Figure 2.7: Adding Non-Activity-Based Costs to Generate the Total Financial Plan

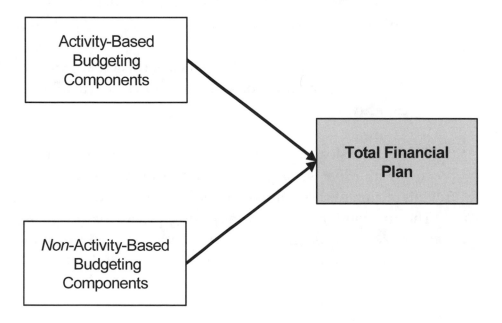

2.3.3 Step 6: Balance Financial Results with Financial Targets

When a financial plan has been prepared, an assessment is made as to whether or not the total projected financial results meet the required targets of the organization. If these targets are not achieved, three options can be pursued, either individually or in combination with one another, as shown in Figure 2.8.[12] These options are:

1. Adjust demand pricing, assuming that the new pricing is compatible with the market,

2. Modify resource costs, including the possibility of outsourcing, and

3. Go back to operational balance and adjust one or more of: demand, consumption rates, or available capacity.

This discussion addresses these options in sequence; however, in a live setting, the sequence of review and the full interaction of these options must be considered.

The first option is that of adjusting prices for products and services. An organization must estimate the impact of an increase or decrease in price on the quantity of demand,

---

[12] A fourth option is to change the targets. However, because the targets are assumed to reflect the organization's strategy, this option is not shown or considered throughout this book.

Figure 2.8: Achieving Financial and Operational Balance

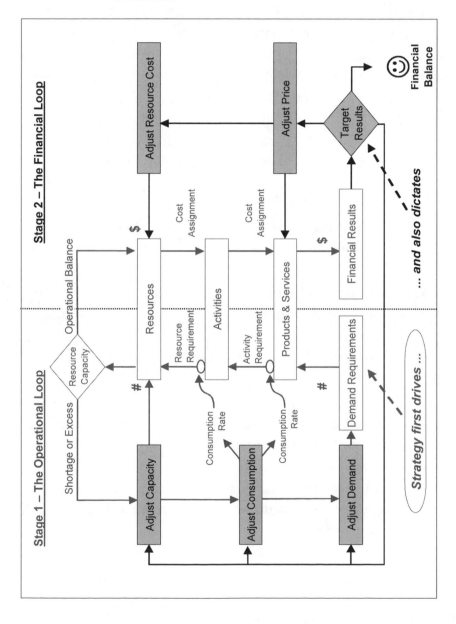

as it is clearly inappropriate (in most cases) to simply assume that, say, a 5% increase in price will result in a 5% increase in revenues. Once the impact on demand of a change in price is estimated, the new quantities must be entered into the operational plan, and the issue of operational balance must be addressed again. Does the new level of demand reach operational balance and, if not, what steps might be taken to achieve the required balance?

The second option is to adjust resource costs (other than by directly changing quantity). Examples of this approach include:

- Re-calibrating shifts to reduce or eliminate current shift premiums or overtime,

- Adopting a two-tier wage structure, where new employees are initially paid less than existing ones,

- Adjusting compensation plans to allow for incentive pay to be more closely tied to organizational results,

- Increasing or decreasing wages to motivate workers to join or leave the organization,

- Paying for skills rather than seniority (assuming that a worker with multiple skills can have the effect of adding capacity),

- Outsourcing to obtain lower costs from more efficient suppliers or reducing excess capacity costs by only paying for what is used,

- Negotiating more favorable energy and other supply contracts, and

- Substituting less expensive materials, providing that other costs (e.g. processing effort or waste) are not increased.

As with the approach of changing prices for products and services, changing resource unit costs might also affect (deliberately or not) resource quantity. If that is the case, the operational plan must be reviewed to ensure that the new level of resource quantity continues to provide operational balance.

The third option is to change one or more of the operational parameters directly:

- Quantity of demand (including mix),

- Activity and/or resource consumption rates, and

- Available capacity.

The Closed-Loop Model shows how changes in these operational parameters can affect resources, required capacity, and ultimately, the financial performance of the organization.   In addition, the Closed-Loop Model demonstrates how changing activity and resource consumption rates, or other operational parameters, can affect the budget. The Closed-Loop Model is the first budget approach to capture these types of links. A change in any of the operational parameters requires management to generate a new operational balance before re-addressing the question of financial balance.

At some point, a satisfactory operational and financial balance will be achieved that meets the strategic requirements of the organization. At this point, a formal budget can be generated in the appropriate format and structure for the organization.

2.3.4 Step 7: Create a Formal Budget

When both operational and financial balance have been achieved, a more formal line-item budget can be created. Such a budget generally includes both activity-based and non-activity-based components. Figure 2.9 provides an overview of the elements that comprise the formal budget.

In some organizations, it may not be necessary to go to this level of detail. The operational and financial plans generated from the Closed-Loop Model may be sufficient to run the business. Alternatively, the formal budget detail may be required but on a less frequent basis. For example, the Closed-Loop Model could be used on a quarterly basis and the detailed formal budget generated annually.

Figure 2.9: Creating the Formal Budget

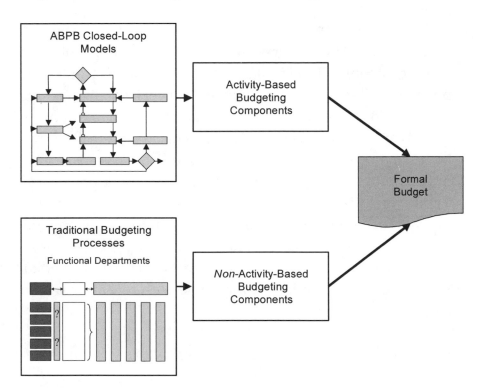

2.4 AN ADDITIONAL CONSIDERATION: EXCESS CAPACITY

One of the key cost management issues is how to handle the cost of excess capacity. The discussion thus far has made the assumption that there is no excess capacity or, if there is, that the amount is insignificant. In this case, the cost of that excess capacity can be treated as a part of product cost without significantly affecting the overall results. In some situations, however, the amount of excess capacity is significant and cannot be reduced in the specific planning period.

One such example is a vehicle assembly plant that can produce 500,000 cars per year, but in the planning phase a volume of only 300,000 is forecast. In this example, the physical facilities cannot be quickly "downsized" to meet the expected demand level. Thus, a substantial amount of excess capacity will remain. This excess capacity will carry a large share of traditionally fixed overhead costs, such as property taxes, building depreciation, heat, light, power, etc. CAM-I regards these costs as expenses of the time period instead of product costs. CAM-I also recommends separating capacity costs into three components: idle, productive, and non-productive capacity (Klammer 1996). The Closed-Loop Model is compatible with this approach to costing excess capacity.

With the fundamentals of the Closed-Loop Model now understood, Chapter 3 provides a detailed example of a Closed-Loop Model and the calculations involved in each step as applied in a service industry organization.

3

CHAPTER

An Application of the Closed-Loop Model

3.1 SUMMARY

To demonstrate how the Closed-Loop Model can be applied, let us consider a real application, one that has been simplified for clarity and ease of calculation. This chapter presents a service industry case: a call center based in the central United States that makes outbound promotional calls to prospective customers (as opposed to one receiving calls, such as an airline reservations center). Each group of calls is referred to as a campaign, such as a campaign to sell a certain product or service. The call center sells campaigns to its clients, providing a guaranteed number of "signed-up" customers. The clients provide a prospect list as well as a script for the call center operators to use in the sales call. The mission of the call center is to provide quality customers at a low cost to its clients, and its organizational strategy is one of aggressive growth.

In building this case, five major assumptions have been made:

1. The planning and budgeting time period is one year,

2. The promotional campaigns are very similar in nature,

3. There is one activity per campaign and one resource for the activity,

4. Senior management has established that a 12% return on gross revenue is the minimum level of acceptable financial performance, and

5. The number of guaranteed "signed-up" customers is achieved and thus there is no penalty cost for not meeting performance targets.

3.2 BASE YEAR, OPERATIONAL AND FINANCIAL BALANCE

Management used the actual operational and financial results from the previous year as the starting point to develop the next year's budget projections. In this example, this prior year is referred to as the *base year*.[13] Thus, the base year's operational consumption rates were **initially** assumed to apply in the next year; these rates could then be used to

---

[13] While a Closed-Loop Model can be designed for almost any time period, this example will use a year for simplicity.

calibrate the Closed-Loop Model and derive the preliminary budget for the next year. The following paragraphs present the calculations for this particular case.

3.2.1 Operational Balance

The derivation of the total resource requirement is shown in Figure 3.1. In the base year, the center conducted 12 campaigns with revenue of $750,000 per campaign. Each campaign required 100,000 outbound calls (the activity consumption rate). Based on this rate, the total activity demand was 1,200,000 calls (12 campaigns x 100,000 calls each). Each call averaged 10 minutes of operator time (the resource consumption rate). The call center calculated a total resource requirement of 200,000 hours of operator time to handle these calls (1,200,000 calls x 10 minutes per call / 60 minutes per hour), as shown below the "Labor" box near the top of Figure 3.1.

Note that the resource consumption rate is measured in *units of time*, minutes per call, resulting in total resource demand also being measured in *units of time*, hours; however, resource supply is measured in *FTEs*.[14] Therefore, management had to convert either the resource consumption rate or the resource supply metric so that they both used the same unit of measure. Therefore, the operator hours were converted to *FTEs*.

---

[14] While it is true that personnel can often be acquired on a part-time basis, such as 0.5 or 0.75 of an FTE (or even on an hourly basis), this example simplifies the issue by assuming whole FTEs.

Figure 3.1: Establishing Operational Balance: Base Year

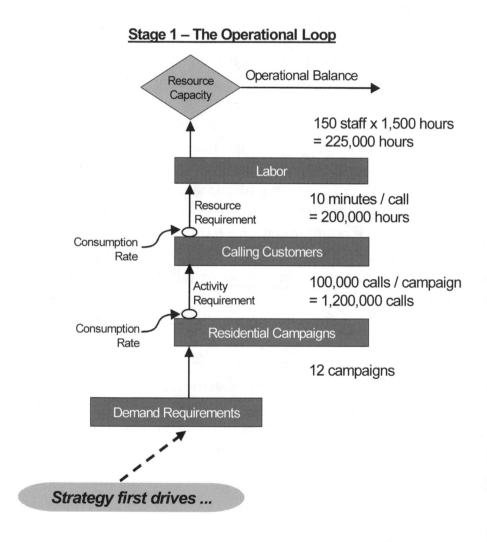

Each employee has a theoretical capacity of 2,080 hours per year (52 weeks per year x 5 days per week x 8 hours per day). From this theoretical level, time for vacation, illness, training, statutory holidays, downtime, etc., should be subtracted to determine available productive capacity. For this example, available productive capacity was assumed to be 1,500 hours per FTE per year. Thus, the center's requirement to handle the base year's volume of 12 campaigns was 133.33 FTEs (200,000 hours of total resource demand / 1,500 hours per year per employee).

In the base year, as shown near the top of Figure 3.1, the center decided to have a staff complement of 150 FTEs, leaving an unused capacity of 16.67 FTEs. The unused capacity was acceptable to management because it enabled the center to respond to short-term unexpected fluctuations in demand and minor seasonal variability without compromising service quality. This decision meant that the 16.67 FTEs were defined as "buffer" rather than "excess" capacity, and as such the cost of these employees can be included in the cost of product/service. With this decision, operational balance had been reached, and the call center achieved its operating goals with the existing resources and parameters.

3.2.2 Financial Balance

Achieving operational balance was the starting point for the financial evaluation. Management then moved to Stage

Figure 3.2: Obtaining Financial Balance: Base Year

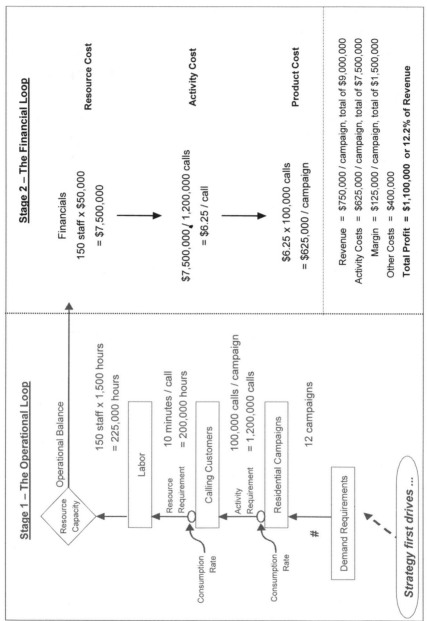

2 of the Closed-Loop Model, reaching financial balance (see Figure 3.2).

First, the total resource requirement was combined with the resource unit cost. In the base year, staff compensation, including salary, benefits, etc., was $50,000 per FTE. Multiplying this figure by the number of FTEs (150) resulted in a total resource cost of $7,500,000. The Closed-Loop Model generated the total resource costs needed to develop the organization's budget. In addition, the underlying calculations were used to generate further detail about individual products, activities, and processes.[15]

In this example, the average activity-based cost of each call was $6.25 (total resource cost / total calls, or $7,500,000 / 1,200,000 = $6.25 per call) and the activity-based cost of each campaign was $625,000 (cost per call x number of calls per campaign, or $6.25 x 100,000 = $625,000). This cost information could then have been used to provide a profitability analysis of each campaign.[16] The ability to perform this type of analysis is a major benefit of the Closed-Loop Model.

At this point, the Activity-Based Budgeting components had been generated for the base year. Additional costs that the center had accounted for outside the Closed-Loop Model were then included in the assessment of financial balance.

---

[15] In a more complex setting with multiple resources, activities, and products, management might provide individual product costs by using tables showing how resources map onto activities and how activities map to products.

[16] In this simplified example, the revenue for each campaign was assumed to be the same and thus all campaigns were equally profitable.

Costs from outside the Closed-Loop Model were as follows:

General manager	$100,000
Facility lease	200,000
Telecom costs	60,000
Other sundry items	40,000
Total non-activity-based costs ("Other Costs" in Figure 3.2)	$400,000

To determine the total profit, management took the sales revenue of $9,000,000 ($750,000 per campaign x 12 campaigns) and subtracted the activity-based costs of $7,500,000 and non-activity-based costs of $400,000. The resulting income statement was as follows:

Sales revenues	$9,000,000
Less: activity-based costs	7,500,000
Less: non-activity-based costs	400,000
Total profit	$1,100,000

In this example, the total profit was $1,100,000 or 12.2% of revenues. As this was in excess of the required target of 12%, the results met the financial requirements and the plan was in financial balance.

These figures represented both planned and actual results, and the center achieved its financial goal with the existing expenditures for resources and operations.

3.3 NEXT YEAR, OPERATIONAL AND FINANCIAL BALANCE, SCENARIO 1

In the next year, the organization committed to continue its strategy of aggressive growth. Marketing confirmed that a sales volume increase of 50%, to 18 campaigns, has been achieved in large part by reducing the price of each campaign to $675,000.

The organization's initial scenario made the simple assumption that the base year's consumption rates can be used to forecast the next year's activity and resource requirements. Based on the consumption rates, the call center will require a total of 300,000 hours of operator resources to handle these calls (18 campaigns x 100,000 calls per campaign x 10 minutes per call / 60 minutes per hour). This requirement translates into 200 FTEs (300,000 hours / 1,500 hours per FTE), as shown in Figure 3.3.

A total of 200 FTEs will be required in the next year as compared with the 150 FTEs required for the base year. Thus, not only would the increased level of demand fully consume the 16.67 buffer FTEs that existed in the base year, but it would also require the hiring of 50 additional employees. In order to achieve operational balance, the center must adjust one or more of available capacity, consumption rates, or demand. Figure 3.4 illustrates that the center chose to achieve operational balance by increasing

Figure 3.3: Generating Resource Requirements: Next Year - Budget Scenario 1, Increase Demand

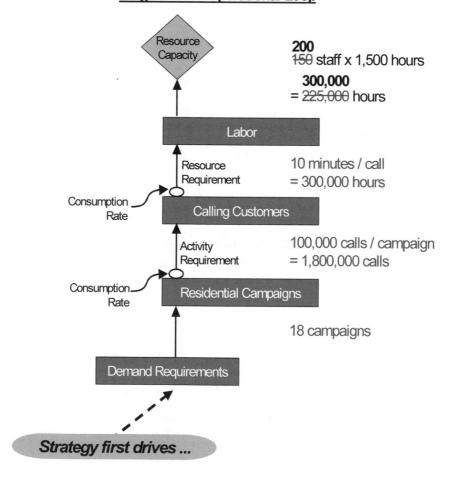

Stage 1 – The Operational Loop

Resource Capacity

200
~~150~~ staff x 1,500 hours

300,000
= ~~225,000~~ hours

Labor

Resource Requirement

10 minutes / call
= 300,000 hours

Consumption Rate

Calling Customers

Activity Requirement

100,000 calls / campaign
= 1,800,000 calls

Consumption Rate

Residential Campaigns

18 campaigns

Demand Requirements

Strategy first drives ...

Figure 3.4: Achieving Operational Balance: Next Year-Budget Scenario 1, Increase Demand

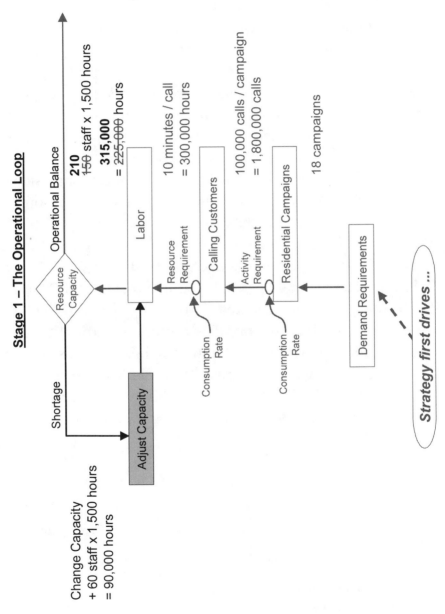

resource capacity.

In this scenario, the center would adjust capacity and plans for a staff complement of 210 FTEs, providing a very small level of buffer capacity (10 FTEs).[17] Assuming that the 60 additional employees could be found, hired, trained, located in the facility, etc., the center would achieve operational balance, because there would be sufficient resources to meet the resource requirements.   Next, management would need to assess whether this operational balance meets the center's financial objectives.

Figure 3.5 provides the basis of the financial analysis in this scenario.   As before, the center combined the resource quantities and costs. The labor pool was now planned to be 210 FTEs. The center also budgeted for a 4% compensation increase for operators, or a total compensation of $52,000 per FTE, generating a total operator resource cost of $10,920,000. The center had now generated the activity-based budget components for this scenario. The center next brought in the forecasts for the "Other Costs" that it handles outside the Closed-Loop Model (also shown in Figure 3.5). These costs also had been updated to reflect the center's continued aggressive strategy and other cost increases projected for the next year.

---

[17] One simplifying assumption in this case is that the 18 campaigns have already been sold, and therefore reducing demand is not a viable option.   In most situations, however, the solution will rarely be so simple. Operational balance will likely only be achieved through combinations of options, such as some additional resource capacity along with some amount of operational improvement.

Figure 3.5: Seeking Financial Balance: Next Year – Budget Scenario 1, Increase Demand

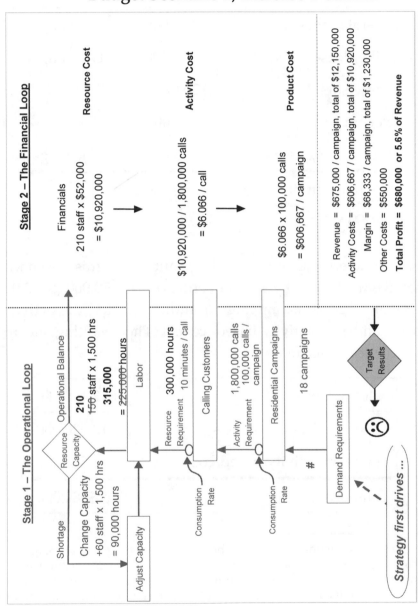

In this scenario, costs from outside the Closed-Loop Model were as follows:

General manager	$100,000	Unchanged
Facility lease	200,000	Unchanged
Supervisors	120,000[18]	
Telecom costs	90,000[18]	
Other sundry items	40,000	Unchanged
Total non-activity- based costs	$550,000	

To determine the total profit for this scenario, management took the sales revenue of $12,150,000 ($675,000 per campaign x 18 campaigns) and subtracted the activity-based and non-activity-based costs. The resulting income statement was as follows:

Sales revenues	$12,150,000
Less: activity-based costs	10,920,000
Less: non-activity-based costs	550,000
Total profit	$680,000

---

[18] Supervisors are now required to help manage the higher campaign and call volumes. Telecom costs increased directly in proportion to the number of campaigns. In some instances, one might also consider an increase in facility lease costs, but this has not been done in this example.

In this scenario, the total profit was $680,000 or 5.6% of revenues, well below the required target of 12%. This level of profitability is not only below the target level, it is also lower than the base year's results! Simply put, these results were not acceptable to management.

Three key events had taken place to generate this unsatisfactory result:

1. Service prices had been reduced by 10% to increase market share.

2. The increase in volume required the organization to add operator staff. Operator costs do not change in direct proportion to volume, but rather change in larger amounts as volume crosses predictable steps; that is, operator costs behave in a manner known as a "step function." Step function costs are fixed across some predictable or known range of volume, but step higher or lower in other volume ranges. In this scenario, the increase in demand had caused the center to "cross" a step.[19]

3. Because of the increase in operator staff, a similar step increase had taken place in the "Other Costs" area. Additional supervisors were hired and telecom costs were also increased.

---

[19] This "step" reflects both resource quantity and resource unit cost. In other words, it is the combination of the increase in compensation ($2,000 / FTE) and the larger number of operators (210 versus 150) that crosses the step.

Because this plan was not in financial balance (the required return on revenue was not met), management was forced to reject it and to seek a new operating plan that would deliver the required results.

3.4 NEXT YEAR, OPERATIONAL AND FINANCIAL BALANCE, SCENARIO 2

Since the initial scenario's result was not acceptable, there are five distinct actions the center could take to move toward financial balance. To achieve balance, management could adjust:

1. Resource costs,

2. Product price,

3. Resource capacity,

4. Activity and/or resource consumption rates, and

5. Demand volume.

These actions are shown in Figure 3.6. Two of these five actions (product price and demand volume) could be immediately ruled out since management had already committed to its clients to provide 18 campaigns in the next year at $675,000 per campaign. However, the other three options must be considered, although the sequence in which

Figure 3.6: Achieving Financial and Operational Balance: Next Year - Budget Scenario 2

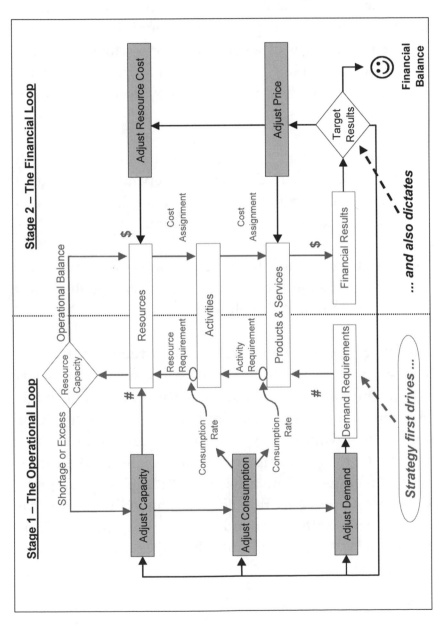

they are considered would be different for each organization. In many cases, no option on its own would result in an operationally and financially balanced plan or budget. Rather, the organization would be required to implement all or parts of several options to achieve balance.

Let's assume that the next option the call center considered was to adjust resource costs. Resource costs are generally of two types:

- **Fixed rate** costs, such as an annual salary or hourly wage rate, where the rate is independent of volume, although the number of resources might be variable and so total cost is linked to volume, or

- **Fixed** costs, where both the rate and resource quantity are independent of volume (or at least within some "relevant range" of volume).

What are the manager's resource cost reduction choices? The first option relates to fixed rate costs, such as the salary paid to employees. To reduce costs, the center might implement a pay reduction initiative, but reducing staff compensation would likely lead to staff turnover, or worse, the inability to hire competent staff at a time when more staff are required. Similarly, a multi-level pay program, where new employees are paid less than existing ones, can easily generate internal friction among employees. Thus, this approach was deferred until the impact of other options is considered.

The second resource cost reduction choice relates to the fixed costs of the center. Changes here are unlikely to solve the manager's problem, at least in the short term, because very little, if any, of the fixed costs are under the immediate and direct influence or control of management.   For example, lease costs are committed on a multi-year basis. The only short-term changeable costs in this area were salaries for the new supervisors and sundry expenses. Assume that the manager saw each of these items as being unavoidable, especially in light of the higher volumes, and therefore other ideas must be considered. In any event, the profit shortfall is so severe that even the complete elimination of all of the "Other Costs" would not deliver financial balance.

The third option is to adjust resource capacity. Scenario 1 demonstrated that capacity changes by themselves are not likely to generate a viable financial plan. In any event, the only variable here is the 10 FTEs of buffer capacity and, in light of the total financial picture, this is a relatively small cost.[20] Therefore, management turned to the final option – adjust consumption rates.

When looking to adjust consumption rates, there are two options to consider: the activity consumption rate and the resource consumption rate.[21] The activity consumption rate

---

[20] This analysis has not considered the option of drawing on management staff to handle the load of some operators. But in this simple example, there are only three managerial employees – the center manager and two supervisors – so the effect would be negligible.

[21] In this analysis, only one of each kind of rate is used, but in a more complex situation, multiple rates, as well as the interaction of those rates, would be reviewed.

is the number of calls per campaign, which historically has been 100,000. As this rate was developed from the base year data and had met the quality levels demanded by customers, management decided that this rate should be left unchanged if at all possible. In some circumstances, the activity consumption rate might even be part of the contract with a customer, and the rate therefore could not be changed without violating those terms. This then leaves management with just one variable to alter: the resource consumption rate, in this example the number of minutes per call.

Process improvement options that would reduce the length of each call include reducing the number of questions, simplifying certain questions, and utilizing automated dialing software so that call center staff would pick up only when a call was answered by a prospective customer. However, the first two approaches might compromise campaign quality and/or standards to which the center might be contractually committed, and are therefore deferred in the short term. Management learned, however, that the parent organization has access to proven automated dialing software and that the center could license it at no incremental cost.

Assume that the automated software could reduce the expected length of each call from 10 minutes to 9 minutes without compromising service levels or the quality of results, and that this operational change was tested and found to be viable. The effect on operational balance of this change in the resource consumption rate is shown in Figure 3.7.

Figure 3.7: The Effect of a Changed Consumption Rate: Next Year - Budget Scenario 2

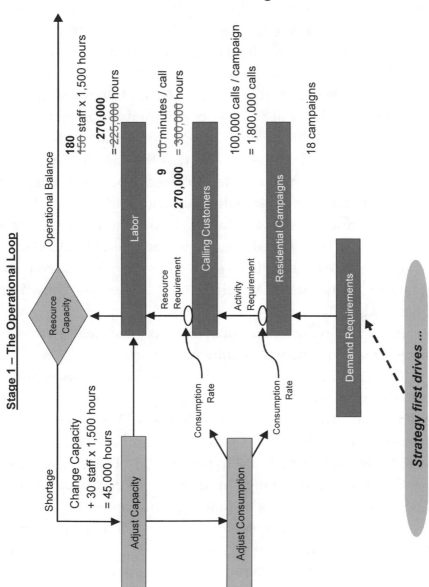

Each of the 18 campaigns would continue to require 100,000 outbound calls, but the average call duration would fall to 9 minutes per call, for a total of 270,000 hours of operator time (1,800,000 calls * 9 minutes per call / 60 minutes per hour) or 180 FTEs (270,000 hours / 1,500 hours per FTE).

If the center felt able to hire 60 additional staff at a compensation level of $52,000 per employee (as planned in Scenario 1), then hiring only 30 additional staff at that wage rate would not be an issue. As was the case in Scenario 1 however, management decided to assess operational balance with some allowance for buffer capacity and so would look to assess results with a total of 40 additional staff, for a buffer of 10 FTEs. This decision yielded operational balance, as the resources supplied (190 FTEs) would exceed the quantity of resources required (180 FTEs), as shown in Figure 3.8.

After achieving operational balance, the next step is to assess financial balance, as shown in Figure 3.9.

The key differences between Scenario 2 and Scenario 1 are the significantly lower activity and product costs in Scenario 2. The activity cost in Scenario 2 is $5.49 per call (versus $6.07 in Scenario 1), and each campaign's direct cost is $548,889 (versus $606,667 in Scenario 1). These lower costs are due *solely* to the change in the resource consumption rate and the resulting impact on staffing requirements.

As Figure 3.9 indicates, the result is in financial balance. Combining the resource requirement of 190 FTEs (actually the resource *decision*, to be specific, as the requirement was

Figure 3.8: The Addition of Buffer Capacity: Next Year - Budget Scenario 2

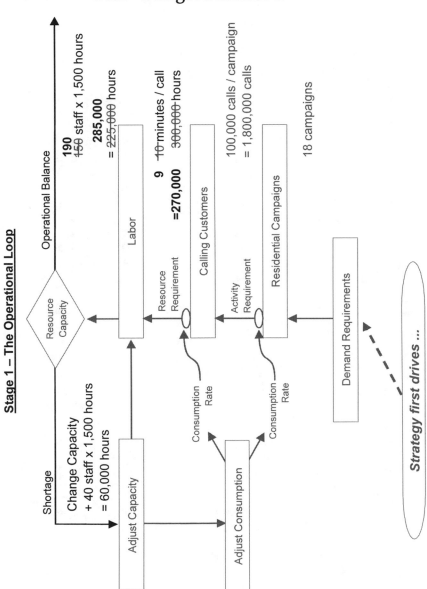

Figure 3.9: Achieving Financial and Operational Balance: Next Year - Budget Scenario 2

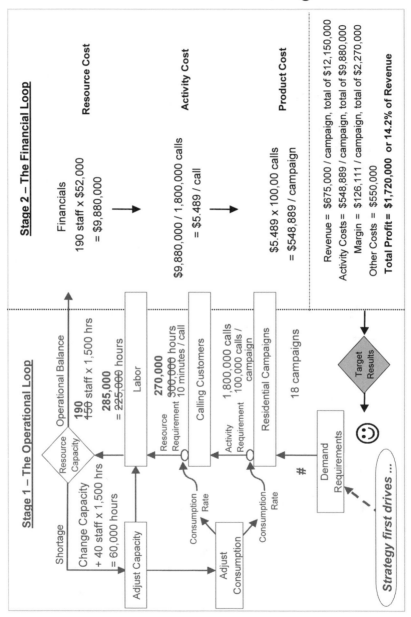

for only 180 FTEs) and the resource cost of $52,000/FTE generated total resource costs of $9,880,000.

As in Scenario 1, costs from outside the Closed-Loop Model totaled $550,000. To determine the total profit, management takes the sales revenue of $12,150,000 ($675,000 per campaign x 18 campaigns) and subtracts the activity-based and non-activity-based costs. The resulting income statement is as follows:

Sales revenues	$12,150,000
Less: activity-based costs	9,880,000
Less: non-activity-based costs	550,000
Total profit	$1,720,000

Scenario 2 yields a total profit of $1,720,000 or a 14.2% return on revenue, well in excess of the desired target. In fact, this level of profitability might enable the center to further reduce prices, perhaps to lock in a higher volume of business for several years to come, or to grow volume beyond 18 campaigns per year. The center must also recognize that the 190 operators are now effectively at capacity, and additional volumes would require additional staff unless further process improvements can be achieved.

In addition to a pricing change, several other operating options are open to management, such as increased staff training, higher wages to allow for hiring better qualified staff, or slightly raising the time per call. As a 12% return on revenue would result in a profit of $1,458,000, management might consider investing up to an incremental $262,000 (the difference between $1,720,000 and $1,458,000) without dropping below the required 12% return on revenue. As long as the desired return on revenue is achieved, the center would be in financial balance.

The center has now achieved both operational and financial balance. If desired, the center could use the detailed activity and resource information to develop line-item, activity-based, or other types of budgets for departments, units, or cost centers.

This simple demonstration of the Closed-Loop Model has shown how Activity-Based Planning and Budgeting can provide a sound basis for decision-making. The next step is to illustrate how the example could be modified to include more than one activity as well as multiple products and services.

3.5 MULTIPLE ACTIVITIES FOR MULTIPLE PRODUCTS AND SERVICES

The previous example described a very simple situation. Real life, of course, is more complicated. An organization offers multiple products and services to its customers and requires multiple activities and resources to deliver them. Products and services share activities and activities share resources. Complexity results largely from the number of relationships and their inter-relationships; however, the individual relationship between one product/service and one activity follows the same pattern as described in the previous example, and is shown in Figure 3.10.

Figure 3.10: Extension of the Closed-Loop Model to Two Activities and Two Services

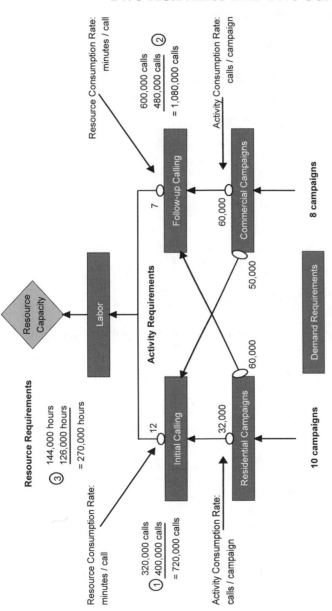

Resource Consumption Rate: minutes / call

600,000 calls
480,000 calls
——————————
= 1,080,000 calls ②

Activity Consumption Rate: calls / campaign

Follow-up Calling

7

Commercial Campaigns

60,000

8 campaigns

Resource Capacity

Labor

Activity Requirements

50,000

Demand Requirements

Initial Calling

12

Residential Campaigns

32,000

60,000

10 campaigns

Resource Requirements

③ 144,000 hours
   126,000 hours
   ————————
   = 270,000 hours

Resource Consumption Rate: minutes / call

① 320,000 calls
   400,000 calls
   ————————
   = 720,000 calls

Activity Consumption Rate: calls / campaign

① 10 residential campaigns at 32,000 initial calls each plus 8 commercial campaigns at 50,000 initial calls each.

② 10 residential campaigns at 60,000 follow-up calls each plus 8 commercial campaigns at 60,000 follow-up calls each.

③ 720,000 initial calls at 12 minutes/call ÷ 60 minutes per hour = 144,000 hours.
1,080,000 follow-up calls at 7 minutes per call ÷ 60 minutes per hour = 126,000 hours.

Adding multiple activities and products requires few modifications to the Closed-Loop Model beyond the additional activities, resources, and products and services. But there are three small changes:

- The individual relationships and consumption rates must be determined,

- Each activity must accumulate the requirements placed on it from each product and service individually, and

- Each activity places its own requirements on the resources it needs. Likewise, each resource must accumulate the requirements placed on it before its operational balance can be evaluated.

In effect, the biggest impact of a more realistic situation is the added complexity to the mathematical calculations required to complete the Closed-Loop Model. In such cases, software algorithms can be effective, as opposed to more manual techniques.

3.6 THE HAZARD OF EXTRAPOLATING ACTIVITY COSTS

Scenario 1 (see Section 3.3 above) can be used to demonstrate why activity costs should not simply be extrapolated from one year to the next to estimate future year expenses.   Extrapolation would have resulted in the following profit forecast:

New sales price per campaign	$675,000
Less prior year activity-based cost per campaign	625,000
Equals gross margin per campaign	50,000
Times number of campaigns	18
Equals total gross margin	900,000
Less new non-activity-based costs	550,000
Total profit	$350,000

While this level of profitability would have been as unacceptable as the profit derived from the Closed-Loop Model in Figure 3.5 ($680,000), the difference is almost 100% of the result of the "extrapolation" ($350,000 versus $680,000). Thus, there is a potential for much larger errors when the extrapolation method is used.   Perhaps more importantly, the actions taken by management to reach financial balance would likely have been much more severe using the extrapolation approach than were actually required in Scenario 2.

The magnitude of the type of error caused by extrapolating data is a function of the change in volume of demand and whether or not "steps" in cost functions are crossed.   Extrapolation assumes that total activity and product/service costs are directly variable with volume, whereas some portion of those costs are "fixed" and that portion can not be determined without application of the Closed-Loop Model.   It is relatively easy to envision a scenario where the extrapolation approach delivers a budget result significantly better than or worse than the Closed-Loop Model. It is equally easy to envision a more dramatic error in which the results of the extrapolation approach are in financial balance whereas the Closed-Loop Model would prove the opposite results (or vice versa).

This chapter has demonstrated an example of the Closed-Loop Model in a relatively simple services industry setting. Readers from the manufacturing and processing industries should be able to modify the example to their particular situations. However, many may feel that the public sector offers a very different situation and may wonder whether or how the Closed-Loop Model can be applied in that particular circumstance.

The next chapter, Chapter 4, deals specifically with two unique government settings and also applies the Closed-Loop Model to a shared services center, which is common to many industries.

4 CHAPTER

Adapting the Closed-Loop Model to Additional Settings

The call center example in the previous chapter demonstrated the Closed-Loop Model in a service-oriented commercial enterprise. This chapter illustrates the robustness of the Closed-Loop Model and how it can be adapted to two different types of government agencies and a shared services setting. In all three settings, applying the Closed-Loop Model requires only minimal modifications, sometimes limited to wording or terminology.[22] These examples keep the framework of the Closed-Loop Model intact and add incremental elements that explain the application of the Closed-Loop Model in each of the additional settings.

4.1 GOVERNMENT COST-RECOVERY AGENCIES

Many government organizations, from the federal to the local level, operate on a cost recovery basis. For example,

---

[22] While the first two sections of this chapter are written from the perspective of, and draw on terminology applicable to, the United States and its various levels of government, the approach and examples are equally applicable to many other countries' public sector environments.

state licensing agencies, military non-appropriated fund instrumentalities, and industrial entities, among others, provide products and services to customers and collect a fee to offset some or all of their costs. Some, but not all, of these organizations also receive limited legislative subsidies that are intended to mitigate the cost of services to customers. These organizations are examples of what is meant by the term *cost-recovery agencies*. Figure 4.1 shows the Closed-Loop Model adapted for such agencies.

Cost-recovery agencies are similar to commercial enterprises in that they generate revenue by producing products or services that are consumed by customers. The main difference between the two is that the goal of cost-recovery agencies is to recover some or all of their costs instead of making a profit. In addition, government agencies are often more highly regulated and almost certainly more politically "supervised" than commercial enterprises. Thus, they may have limited flexibility to *rapidly* adjust their resource capacity, consumption rates, or consumer prices in reaction to changes in demand or other business parameters.

In a cost-recovery agency, the Closed-Loop Model begins with a mandate and a mission for the agency. This mandate and mission allows the agency's managers to establish a strategy, and, as is the case in the commercial sector, this strategy influences the demand requirements for the agency. Then, following the Closed-Loop Model, the agency works on achieving operational balance.

Demand requirements determine the amount of work required, and in turn, the resources required to perform that

Figure 4.1: The Closed-Loop Model for Government Cost-Recovery Agencies

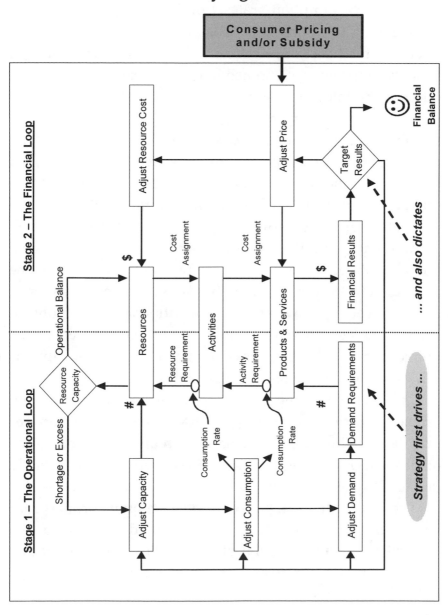

work. As in the commercial sector, operational balance can be achieved through adjustments to any or all of resource capacity, consumption rates, or quantity of demand. Managers in the public sector, as in the private sector, can affect the total cost of resources or change capacity through process improvement, outsourcing, privatization, and/or other methodologies.

The dissimilarity to the commercial sector appears mainly in the financial balance stage and is mostly caused by differences in terminology and perspective rather than a difference in the substance of the Closed-Loop Model. Once operational balance is achieved and the financial results are calculated, the cost-recovery agency must adjust its budget in different ways than those available to the commercial sector.   Specifically, price adjustments may not be immediately or directly possible in government, as price may be set by law or heavily influenced by political considerations and sensitivities. Nevertheless, even in the public sector, adjusting price remains one of the options towards achieving financial balance.

The user fees earned by cost-recovery agencies may not provide sufficient funds to cover the full costs of the services provided. This shortfall creates a requirement for some other form of funding for the cost-recovery agency, broadly defined here as a *subsidy*.

These subsidies can be fixed dollar amounts or may vary with demand volume. Increases or decreases to the subsidies can have a similar effect to adjusting price, in that severe demands for resources could curtail government's desire to provide the service and directly affect the level of resources available to generate sufficient capacity.   The additional "box" outside the Closed-Loop on the right side of Figure 4.1 shows that price adjustments can be made at the consumer price level and/or the subsidy level.   This simply means that changes in the subsidy level affect the unit price requirement, or vice-versa.   Additional budget funds may be made available for the subsidy if the consumer-pricing component is insufficient to meet the total budget requirement.

Adjusting the consumer price (variable fees charged) or the level of subsidy available (whether variable or fixed) are the primary options open to cost-recovery agencies for bringing the Closed-Loop Model into financial balance. Although the terminology differs from that used in the commercial sector, the methods employed are similar (if not identical) and the result is the same.

4.2 GOVERNMENT PROGRAM AGENCIES

Other government organizations are funded either by federal or state legislatures, or local or regional governments through appropriation processes, and are termed *government program agencies*. These types of organizations generally do not receive or earn fees for the services they offer, although in some cases fees may cover a relatively small portion of the organization's total costs.

While in some instances program agencies provide identifiable or tangible services, in many other situations their "services" are not services at all; rather, they provide an outcome or "capability" that may or may not be used. For example, the United States Department of Defense, as a program agency, receives appropriations in order to pay the costs of personnel, training, maintenance, etc. so that it is capable of meeting its mission of defending the United States *if called upon*. This is a significantly different environment from the commercial example described in Chapter 3 and from the cost-recovery agency example presented previously in this chapter. However, the Closed-Loop Model remains applicable, as will be discussed below. The same elements could be applied to other government organizations, such as fire and police departments, although the terminology may differ slightly.

One of the authors of this book has recently worked with an agency of the United States Department of Justice. This agency has employed the Closed-Loop Model and broader ABPB Process to assist in coping with changes in demand for services following the events of September 11th, 2001 ("9-11"). The agency assists in performing aspects of individual background investigations, collecting fees for the service from individuals, businesses, and other government agencies; although the agency charges user fees for its services, these fees represent only about 15% of total costs and therefore the agency is considered a "Program" agency for purposes of the Closed-Loop Model. Legislation passed subsequent to "9-11" has had the expected effect of significantly increasing demand for the agency's services.

The agency's use of the Closed-Loop Model focused primarily on achieving operational balance, in order to be able to continue providing timely responses to requests for assistance. This meant being able to accurately predict the incremental human and other resources that would be required to meet the expected – and actual – increase in demand. Once these requirements were established, the agency was then able to cost the total requirement in order to **ensure that unit transaction costs fell within the current fee and appropriation structure.** If they had not, the agency would have had to negotiate with its parent organization to determine if the additional costs would be covered by additional appropriations or require an increase in the fees charged.

Figure 4.2 shows the Closed-Loop Model for a government program agency, specifically a military organization.

Unlike cost-recovery agencies, program agencies have unique features in both the operational and financial stages of the Closed-Loop. For a program agency, such as the United States Department of Defense, the starting point for the Closed-Loop Model is "readiness," which drives the agency's strategy. This is shown through the addition of the "Readiness" box outside the Closed-Loop Model on the left side of Figure 4.2. Like all other organizations, the strategy determines the demand requirements for the agency.

A difference from the commercial sector is that demand requirements in program agencies are sometimes expressed in non-commercial units. For example, in a military unit, demand requirements might be expressed as a readiness level, deployment capability, or a similar such description, expressed as a composite estimate such as a percentage or tier. The additional "Operational Level" box outside the

Figure 4.2: The Closed-Loop Model for Government Program Agencies

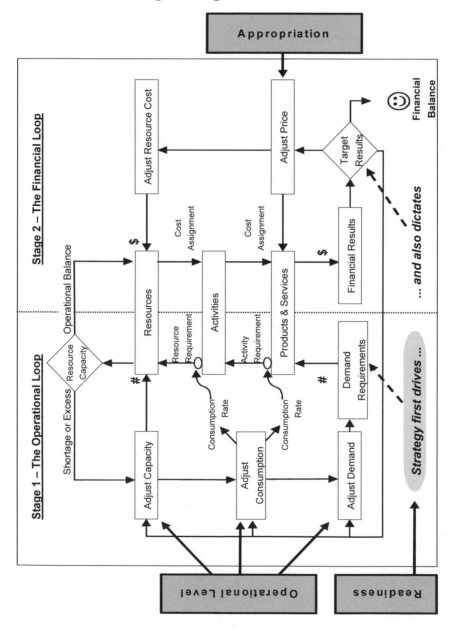

Closed-Loop Model, on the left side of Figure 4.2, implies that changes in operational levels, necessary to meet the readiness requirement, may cause adjustments in demand, consumption rates, and/or capacity in order to achieve operational balance for the organization.

The readiness requirement may also cause the unit to assess the number of exercises or other training activities required to achieve the needed capability. The unit's needed capability, in turn, requires activities to be performed in order to achieve that capability. For a military unit, these activities might include conducting planning, maintaining equipment, transporting personnel and equipment, conducting training, evaluating results, etc. These activities drive individual and aggregate resource requirements, including the unit and support mix, number and types of equipment miles, and training ranges and range days.

A military unit's resource capacity might be expressed in terms compatible with the requirement: it has a certain number of *funded* equipment usages (miles, hours, etc.) available and is provided a share of available training range time, or has an available number of training days. If the unit does not have sufficient quantities of any of the resource elements, its first option is to request more resources or a different mix of resources. The unit's training program may drive the consumption rate or level of effort the unit expends in performing the activities that consume these resources. Should the number of resources be insufficient, then a unit can adjust its training, either by limiting the number of exercises, their duration, their intensity, or their objectives, to consume fewer vehicle miles, range days, training days, etc., as required to balance demand with capacity. If a balance cannot be reached, then changes to readiness levels and capability will result.

On the financial side, "price" may not be applicable as military organizations (and other appropriation funded government organizations) do not generally sell their services, though there may be some exceptions. However, just as price can be used as a tool to adjust demand requirements for a commercial organization's products and services, the amount of government appropriation places limits on the number of exercises or training activities a unit can perform. In this example, the additional "Appropriation" box outside the Closed-Loop Model, on the right side of Figure 4.2, shows that "price" adjustments to budget funding are made available as appropriations. If the appropriated amount cannot be modified, then the unit can attempt to adjust its resource costs, though this may prove very difficult to do in many environments because of a variety of constraints. Consequently, adjustments to operational levels may be required to achieve overall balance — a classic example of how the Closed-Loop Model works.

The examples in Sections 4.1 and 4.2 demonstrate how leaders and managers operating in different types of government environments can apply the Closed-Loop Model with minimal changes. The limitations government agencies face are mostly of terminology and timing — they have limited flexibility to react to changes in the near term — rather than applicability of the Closed-Loop Model.

4.3 SHARED SERVICES SETTINGS

Organizations in many industries are transforming their business models to improve quality and profitability. In some cases, these transformations are using the concept of shared services to optimize the cost base and, at the same time, to improve internal service delivery.

In a shared services setting, common processes are taken out of multiple business units and combined into a separate organization, usually at the corporate (or parent organization) level; these organizations are referred to as Shared Services Centers. Implementing the shared services concept can provide significant cost savings based on economies of scale, improved efficiency, and higher levels of service within the organization. Typical examples of common processes might be accounting, information technology, human resources, facilities, and procurement. A shared services center, when executed effectively, allows each business unit to focus on its core competencies because another group provides the services common to the operating units. From a cost or budgeting perspective, shared services organizations are similar to cost-recovery agencies in that the goal is not necessarily to make a profit, but rather to recover all costs.[23]

---

[23] Shared services centers may be internal to an organization, and in these cases can be cost-recovery units or profit-making units, as the overall organization deems appropriate. Such internal shared services centers may also offer their services to third parties, in a profit-seeking structure. In other cases, organizations sub-contract or outsource certain business processes to external entities, which likely operate as profit-seeking shared services centers.

Traditionally, in most shared services environments, the periodic budgeting process is an exercise in guesswork. The shared services manager estimates the volume and level (e.g. response time) of each service required for the next budget period to satisfy all of the business units served by the center, and then attempts to manage resources according to that estimate. In reality, the estimated level of each service is a best guess, generally based on the previous period's data.

In more advanced environments, the shared services center and each supported business unit agree on a Service Level Agreement (SLA). Such SLAs specifically define each of the services provided for the specified time period. They usually also incorporate service levels, prices, dispute resolution terms, etc. In such agreements, each business unit customer usually guarantees a certain volume or range of volume for each service required. In some organizations, a business unit manager may be allowed to contract with an external provider for some or all of the services available through the shared services center. Doing so however usually has to be justified as providing a significant cost saving or increase in quality.

Figure 4.3 shows how the Closed-Loop Model can be applied in the shared services setting to improve the budget process.

The overall starting point remains the strategy of each business unit that is a customer of the shared services center; each unit will prepare or update its strategy and thus derive its own demand requirements. For the shared services center, the starting point for initiating its own Closed-Loop Model is estimating demand by aggregating the volume of

Figure 4.3: The Closed-Loop Model for Shared Services

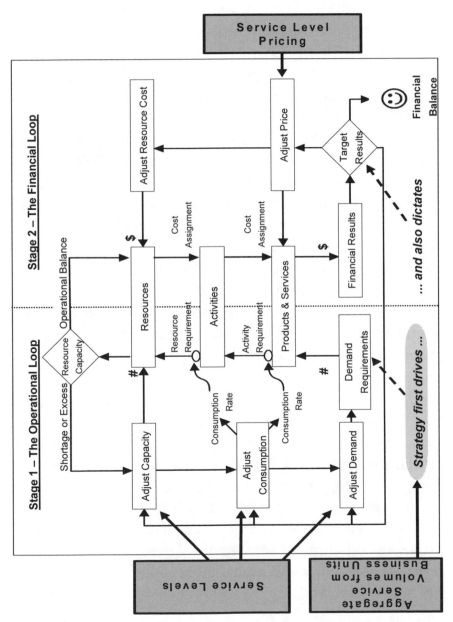

services required from the various business units. To reach operational balance, the level of service provided may also need to be adjusted in addition to (or in conjunction with) changes to demand, consumption rates, or capacity, as shown through the "Service Level" box outside the Closed-Loop Model, on the left side of Figure 4.3. Financial balance is achieved by adjusting the pricing in the SLAs as depicted by the "Service Level Pricing" box outside the Closed-Loop Model, on the right side of Figure 4.3, or adjusting resource costs as in other applications of the Closed-Loop Model.

As a specific example of a shared services setting, consider an information technology data center where demand requirements are obtained from the various business units that use the center. Examples of the services provided by such a center could be transactions, internet or intranet access, customized reports, or desktop support. Some of the activities required to support these demands might be transaction processing, printing, maintenance, programming, or help-line. Examples of metrics used to calculate consumption rates could include number of transactions, number of lines of print, lines of code, number of PC users, number and length of calls, etc. Finally, examples of resources required could be CPU computing power, printers, gigabytes of data storage, number of PCs, hours of programming, or number of support staff personnel.

As shared services center managers plan and modify processes and infrastructure, and assign resources to execute operational and financial plans, they frequently face the following challenges:

- How to reduce the cost (and hence price) of non-strategic processes, particularly high-volume ones,

- How to offer high quality services, on time, at a competitive price,

- How to adjust capacity to respond to the volume fluctuations caused by the business units,

- How to apply a consistent transfer-pricing algorithm across the various businesses for the services provided, and

- How to cost and price new service offerings.

Shared services center managers are discovering that ABPB, as described by the Closed-Loop Model, can be used to establish a framework that provides the predictive cost information required to meet these challenges.

This chapter completes Part 1 of this book. We have described the essentials of the ABPB Closed-Loop Model and have demonstrated how it functions in several common organizational environments.

Part 2 of the book describes how an organization can create its initial Closed-Loop Model, spread it throughout the organization, and turn it into a self-sustaining ABPB Process.

PART 2

IMPLEMENTING THE ACTIVITY-BASED PLANNING AND BUDGETING PROCESS

5 CHAPTER

An Overview of Part 2

Now that the basic Closed-Loop Model has been described, this part of the book turns to the more practical issue of how to implement it. This chapter provides an overview of the implementation process, while the next four chapters describe the steps required to build Closed-Loop Models for an organization's units and ultimately to turn all of the unit models into the self-sustaining, organization-wide ABPB Process.

The CAM-I ABPB Interest Group advocates the use of sound project management practices as the means to achieve "discipline and focus" within an organization. Each implementation of the ABPB Process is planned, executed, and controlled as an *ABPB Project*, with a completed Closed-Loop Model, such as the one developed in Chapter 3, as the deliverable. A project is defined as a "temporary endeavor undertaken to create a unique product or service."[24] The structure of the Closed-Loop Model, its content, and any lessons learned from the previous projects should serve as inputs to the next project. With each successful ABPB Project, measurable progress is made towards

---

[24] Project Management Institute. 2000. *A Guide to the Project Management Book of Knowledge*. Newtown, PA: Project Management Institute, 4.

standardizing the systems and processes that can lead to a mature and sustainable ABPB Process.

The ABPB Process provides an organization with the knowledge, capabilities, abilities, and formal processes required to predict the resources needed and the monetary effects of variations in demand and consumption rates in a reliable, repeatable, and maintainable fashion. This end-state is achieved through the recurring deployment of ABPB Projects that collectively form the *ABPB Implementation Program*, shown in Figure 5.1.[25] A program is defined as a "group of projects managed in a coordinated way to obtain benefits not available from managing them individually" and that may "include an element of on-going operations."[26]

As more ABPB Projects are completed, the emphasis shifts from project management to program management, and ultimately to process management. The transition occurs in three stages. The first is the creation of the Closed-Loop Model, the calculation engine, for a unit of the organization, as depicted by the "APBP Pilot" box in Figure 5.1. The second is the addition of supporting elements that institutionalize the updating of the Closed-Loop Model and fully integrate it into the organization; this is depicted by the "ABPB Expansion" and "ABPB Institutionalization" boxes in

---

[25]   In Figure 5.1, and throughout this book, the term "iteration" refers to the generation of a Closed-Loop Model with different or new data, such as the two scenarios used in Chapter 3, with the ultimate objective of the iterations being a balanced Model.

[26]   Project Management Institute. 2000. *A Guide to the Project Management Book of Knowledge.* Newtown, PA: Project Management Institute, 10.

Figure 5.1: The ABPB Implementation Program

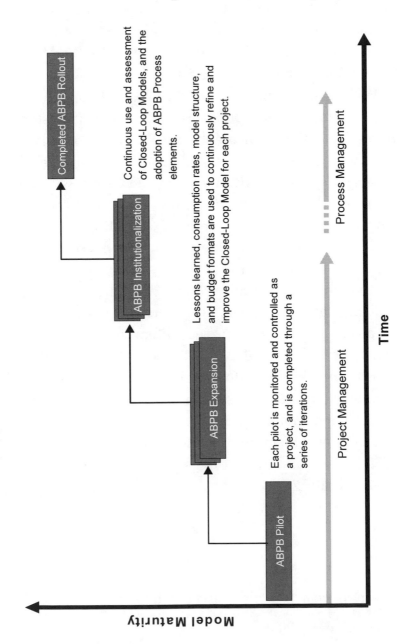

Figure 5.1.   At this point the Closed-Loop Model becomes the ABPB Process for that unit.   The final stage is the expansion of the Closed-Loop Model and ABPB Process to other units in the organization, as shown by the "Completed ABPB Rollout" box in Figure 5.1.

Within the framework of the Closed-Loop Model, good project management practices form the cornerstone of a successful ABPB Implementation Program.   Ultimately, the Closed-Loop Model should become an integral part of ongoing operation through standardized systems and processes.   Reaching maturity, however, does take time and effort.   Good project management — putting first things first — can start an organization on the journey in a systematic manner.

Knowing that projects are essential to the ABPB Implementation Program, an organization should also have an awareness of the project lifecycle to be successful. Understanding where ABPB Project activities fit into the project lifecycle allows for an appreciation of the complexity of getting the program off the ground and the value of the project management approach.

The project lifecycle consists of five phases:[27]

- Initiating,

- Planning,

---

[27] Adapted from Project Management Institute. 2000. *A Guide to the Project Management Book of Knowledge*. Newtown, PA: Project Management Institute.

- Executing,

- Controlling, and

- Closing.

Figure 5.2 depicts a project lifecycle template with representative activities for each phase.

While the five phases in each project are generic, it is the application of the activities shown in Figure 5.2 that is unique to ABPB. Details on the unique aspects of ABPB Projects, such as the cost-reducing aspect of using some ABCM information, will be given in Chapters 6 - 9.

During each phase, a formal assessment that addresses cost, timeline, and scope of the project should be produced. Using this assessment, at each milestone or phase a decision is made to continue, modify, abandon, or postpone the project. While each phase may incorporate multiple milestones for planning purposes, each has a concluding milestone, as described in detail below.

Initiating   Includes describing the need for the project, gathering supporting information, establishing goals and objectives, estimating initial project resource requirements, creating a project charter, developing the communications plan, and obtaining formal sponsorship and a project champion. The phase is complete with the approval of the project charter.

Figure 5.2: Managing an ABPB Implementation Project

Initiating	Planning	Executing	Controlling	Closing

• Describe Need
• Gather Information
• Establish Goals, Objectives
• Estimate Resources
• Develop Communication Plan
• Enlist Project Champion
• Create Project Charter
	• Select Project Manager
	• Institute Internal Procedures
	• Identify Pilot Site
	• Form and Educate Team
	• Develop Detailed Project Plan
	  • Milestones
	  • Deliverables
	  • Risk Mitigation
	• Identify Data Sources
	• Develop Project Evaluation Approach
		• Activate Communication Plan
		• Activate Detailed Project Plan
		  • Make Model Assumptions
		  • Identify Data Sources
		  • Build Model
			• Monitor Milestones
			• Monitor Resources
			• Resolve Problems
				• Finalize Deliverables
				• Complete Documentation
				• Evaluate Project
				• Capture Lessons Learned
				• Debrief Project Team
				• Transfer Model Responsibility

End of Phase: Formal Approval of Charter	End of Phase : Approval of Final Project Plan	End of Phase : Model Built and Debugged	End of Phase : N/A – Ongoing Throughout Project	End of Phase : Acceptance of Final Project Charter

Organizational Effort

Planning   Includes selecting a project manager, instituting internal procedures, finding an implementation site,[28] forming and educating the project team, planning for risks and developing risk mitigation strategies, developing the project plan, and, if required, selecting automated tools or software to assist with the effort. The phase is complete with the conclusion of training for the core team and the approval of the final project plan by the necessary authority.

Executing   Includes training beyond the ABPB core team to include cross-functional units, functions, and staff associated with the effort as defined in the communication plan. Major tasks in this phase are quantifying and forecasting demand for products or services, and estimating the upcoming year's consumption rates. The phase is complete with an operationally and financially balanced model describing products and services, the necessary activities to produce those products and services, and the resources required to perform those activities.

---

[28]   Although a pilot site is not required, it is highly recommended and thus shown in Figure 5.2. A pilot is a sound, widely accepted means of mitigating risk and providing team and organizational education.

Controlling   Includes the activities of the project manager through all phases of the project. The project manager directs the team. This phase is ongoing until the Closing phase is complete, although the level of effort may decline substantially upon the completion of the Executing phase.

Closing   Includes the presentation of the final deliverables to the sponsor and possibly executive management, including any documentation and lessons learned. The project team is de-briefed and then may be assigned to other projects. This final phase is complete with the sponsor's acceptance of the finished Closed-Loop Model.

Based on an understanding of how good project management processes can enhance the ABPB Implementation Program, the balance of Part 2 of this book delves into the details.

Chapter 6   Builds upon the basics of project management to discuss the tactical level of Initiating and Planning an ABPB Project, and offers a "Ten Step" guide for orchestrating these phases.

Chapter 7   Moves from the tactical to the operational level for developing a Closed-Loop Model and addresses issues such as understanding the planning horizon, using the Closed-Loop Model building blocks, collecting the necessary data, and linking all the data together.

Chapter 8   Discusses how to use a Closed-Loop Model to manage the business and describes the key levers that can affect results.

Chapter 9   Focuses on how to implement and sustain the final ABPB Process.

These four chapters provide the information needed to successfully initiate, plan, execute, control, and close the implementation of the projects, as well as how to use and analyze the output of the Closed-Loop Models. While these chapters do not specifically follow the phases described in Figure 5.2, they do follow that approach in broad principle.

The final two chapters in this second part of the book deal with advanced issues.

Chapter 10   Provides additional details on several key elements of the Closed-Loop Model: defining and forecasting demand, measuring consumption rates, and understanding complex activity interactions.

Chapter 11   Discusses data management and the architecture of an ABPB system.

6 CHAPTER

Initiating and Planning an ABPB Project

To become an integral part of an organization's strategic objectives, the newly christened ABPB Implementation Program should be planned, developed, marketed, and managed to achieve buy-in and support for any additional resources needed. Thus, prior to initiating the component projects of the Program, a systematic approach to the Initiating and Planning phases should be taken.

This chapter describes ten steps to Initiating and Planning each individual ABPB Implementation Project, recognizing that many of these steps are standard across most types of projects. These ten steps help to define and control the Initiating and Planning phases. In addition to the guidelines in this chapter, the Project Management Book of Knowledge (PMBOK®), published annually by the Project Management Institute (www.pmi.org), should be referred to as a source for general information on project management.

A successful *program* first requires that its component *projects* also be viewed as successful. In this context, "successful" means that the project:

- Deliverables meet the business objectives that the project was designed to meet,

- Results are accepted and used by management and project sponsors,

- Participants are enthusiastic about both the project itself and its results, and

- Efforts receive the support of management and users to extend the project to other parts of the organization.

The CAM-I ABPB Interest Group has identified a logical series of steps which should be followed in the first two phases of each ABPB project.

Initiating Phase

Step 1: Understand the strategy to support the goals of the organization.

Step 2: Identify the time and resources required for the effort.

Step 3: Draft a communication plan.

Step 4: Develop a project charter.

Step 5: Enlist a project champion for the effort.

Planning Phase

Step 6: Select an appropriate project pilot site.

Step 7: Develop the project plan, listing all associated milestones.

Step 8: Quantify risks and develop risk mitigation plans.

Step 9: Identify the required data sources.

Step 10: Develop a project evaluation plan.

6.1 INITIATING AN ABPB PROJECT

6.1.1 Step 1: Understand the Strategy to Support the Goals of the Organization

As with any project, understanding the strategy and goals of the organization is of critical importance. The project management team must make sure that each ABPB Project fits into the organization's strategy. For example, if part of the strategy is to improve workforce flexibility, the Closed-Loop Model should address labor interchangeability. Crafting the implementation goal to fit the organization's strategy is essential to project success. Doing so requires anticipating who will use the information generated, for what purpose the information will be used, and for what strategies the information will support. The "who" element of an organization's strategy drives the expected use of the resulting information, and thus shapes the degree of granularity of the Closed-Loop Model as well as other aspects of scope and structure. Also, understanding the purpose for which the information is required allows the project team to anticipate data integration requirements and limitations, and greatly enhances the project's long-term usefulness.

6.1.2 Step 2: Identify the Time and Resources Required for the Effort

The ABPB Implementation Team is the group that performs the work during all phases of the ABPB Implementation Project. For smaller organizations, the project team may include only one or two people, but for large organizations the team might consist of many representatives from several functional departments and the modeled site(s). Contributions from multiple functional areas, such as information systems, operations, and finance bring different skills to the table, provide buy-in, and facilitate the transfer of information and ideas relevant to ABPB across multiple groups within the organization. The manager of the ABPB Implementation Project should encourage functional managers to provide their best and brightest individuals for the project team to maximize the likelihood of success.

Initially, many of the people acting as key points of contact to the team, and even the team members themselves, may be unfamiliar with the concepts of ABPB. The project manager is responsible for training and educating the entire team. The key elements for this knowledge and training can be found throughout this book.

6.1.3 Step 3: Draft a Communication Plan

A communication plan provides structure and timelines for regular communication to project stakeholders, lays out who needs what information, and identifies the frequency with which each recipient will receive that information. A communication plan structures the:[29]

> ...process required to ensure timely and appropriate generation, collection, dissemination, storage, and ultimate disposition of project information.   It provides the critical links among people, ideas, and information necessary for success. Everyone involved in the project must be prepared to send and receive communications, and must understand how the communications in which they are involved as individuals affect the project as a whole.

The communication plan should be developed prior to project initiation. Once the effort begins, the hectic pace of

---

[29]   Project Management Institute. 2000. *A Guide to the Project Management Book of Knowledge*. Newtown, PA: Project Management Institute, 117.

the project often does not allow time for reflection and scheduling time for communication to those who may be most affected by the project. Committing to a timeline and to content development early in the process is far easier than scrambling to figure out what to do later.

For the communication plan, consider, at a minimum:

- **Creating a project "white paper"** - The white paper may be as simple as a copy of the project charter that is provided to a few key individuals, or as detailed as a targeted brief provided numerous times to several different groups of stakeholders. A white paper helps to manage and communicate the expectations and goals of the project throughout the organization. When creating a white paper for this purpose, strengths, weaknesses, opportunities, and threats (the SWOT framework) can often be a useful approach.

- **Providing periodic status reports** - Depending on the scope and duration of the effort, regularly scheduled and consistent information on tasks achieved, work in process, and problems or unresolved issues keeps the project on the minds of participants as well as stakeholders. Set a regular schedule for issuing status reports and follow through with that schedule.

- **Publishing project results** - In addition to the submission of the budget, honestly critique the effort and communicate the successes and potential improvements for the program going forward.

6.1.4 Step 4: Develop a Project Charter

The project charter is used to formally establish the project within the organization and provides the project manager with the necessary authority from management to proceed with the project. At a minimum, the charter should outline the business need for the ABPB Process, the expected outcomes of the pilot and expansion projects, the timeline or duration of the initial (and possibly ongoing) effort, the program office or manager assigned to the effort, and the roles and responsibilities of participants. The project charter should be approved by a high level authority, not the project manager. The charter carries with it the necessary authority to allow the project manager to open doors and complete the project.

The naming of a project manager may be the most critical aspect in the launch of the project and thus may be done earlier in the Initiating phase. The project manager should be well-respected in the organization, be knowledgeable about the issues and objectives of the business unit, and be able to form and lead a cross-functional team to project completion.

6.1.5 Step 5: Enlist a Project Champion for the Effort

The project champion is the senior executive whose attitude and enthusiasm legitimizes the effort and galvanizes the project team and cross-functional managers to engage with the program. The project champion motivates and enables the project team members and engages the organization.   The project champion helps the project manager overcome obstacles and communicates the benefits of the project throughout the organization.   In turn, the project manager conveys to the project champion the project status and facilitates his or her involvement in the communication campaign.   The project champion should have sufficient stature in the organization to drive the project forward despite the inevitable challenges that will be encountered.

6.2 PLANNING AN ABPB PROJECT

6.2.1 Step 6: Select an Appropriate Project Pilot Site

Like many business initiatives, the ABPB Process is commonly introduced to the organization through a project *pilot* or proof of concept.   The purpose of a pilot is to demonstrate the benefits of the ABPB Process while uncovering challenges and risks, and generating tips for future implementations.   Throughout the project pilot, it is important to catalog these issues.   Along with this catalog, a plan of action to overcome and minimize any risks that are identified should be established.   Similarly, the success or failure of specific actions should also be documented for future reference.

The selection of the project pilot site should be based on a number of critical success factors.   Because the project pilot is a learning process for everyone involved, the project manager generally selects the site that offers the greatest reward with the lowest risk. When selecting a project pilot site, the following should be considered:

- **Well-Defined Products and Services** – Can the site clearly define the products/services it provides to its customers? Does it currently measure the quality and quantity of those products/services?

- **Maturity of Resource and Activity Drivers** – Does the site, either through activity-based modeling or other engineering and/or service studies, understand the relationship between its products and the activities required to produce them, and the resources consumed by those activities?

- **Manageable Scope** – Is the site small enough to permit the project team to model the activities and drivers within the allotted timeframe? Is the project scope itself manageable to ensure successful completion? Conversely, is the site sufficiently large and complex to provide the team and the organization with a broad learning experience with ABPB?

- **Potential Benefits** – What are the potential benefits, or returns, to the organization from the modeled site, including leveragable knowledge?

- **Level of Skill** – Do the site managers have any previous knowledge of activity-based costing or capacity management concepts?

- **Level of Will** – Does the site desire to assist the team with the project? Are participants willing? Are they apt to use the data provided by the Closed-Loop Model?

Arranging these considerations in a matrix can help the project team choose the project pilot site. For example, potential sites can be ranked with scores from 1 (lowest) to 5 (highest) based on management judgments. The scores can then be placed into a matrix, such as the following:

Selection Criteria	Site #1	Site #2	Site #3
Well-Defined Products and Services	5	3	1
Maturity of Resource and Activity Drivers	2	4	1
Manageable Scope	3	3	5
Potential Benefits	2	4	2
Level of Skill	3	2	4
Level of Will	2	4	5
Total	17	20	18

In this example, it appears that Site #2 is the most promising possibility for the project pilot site, with a high score of 20. A matrix approach can be used to select each succeeding project site. Similar questions should be asked for each potential site, although some of the questions and the relative importance of each answer may change. For example, while it is highly likely that the most complex and least willing business unit will not be the project pilot site, the question of whether that unit is analyzed second, fifth, or last is a more open one.

6.2.2 Step 7: Develop the Project Plan, Listing All Associated Milestones

A project plan formalizes how and with what resources the Closed-Loop Model will be developed. First, a *Work Breakdown Structure* (WBS) is produced through several iterations, each providing a greater level of detail. A WBS is a decomposition of the actions required to meet each deliverable. Each element in the WBS describes a specific task to be accomplished, along with task dependencies, predecessors, and resource requirements. Additionally, milestones are described and defined in the WBS. A milestone is a significant event in the project, usually the completion of a deliverable.[30] Finally, a project plan review and analysis should be conducted which includes such elements as critical path identification and a thorough review of the assumptions associated with each task (e.g. duration to complete task, resource scheduling, etc.)

---

[30] Ibid, 203.

6.2.3 Step 8: Quantify Risks and Develop Risk Mitigation Plans

The risks involved in an ABPB Project, be it in a single site or organization-wide, can be minimized by first identifying the major risks in the project and formally creating action plans to address and overcome these risks.

Project risk management is defined as:

1. **Risk Management Planning** – deciding how to approach and plan the risk management activities for the project.

2. **Risk Identification** – determining which risks might affect the project and documenting their characteristics.

3. **Qualitative Risk Analysis** – performing a qualitative analysis of risks and conditions to assess their potential effects on project objectives.

4. **Quantitative Risk Analysis** – measuring the probability and consequences of risks and estimating their implications for project objectives.

5. **Risk Response Planning** – developing procedures and techniques to enhance opportunities and reduce threats to the project's objectives.

6. **Risk Monitoring and Control** – monitoring residual risks, identifying new risks, executing risk reduction plans, and evaluating their effectiveness throughout the project life cycle.[31]

One common approach to risk management is to require the project manager or project team to develop a risk management template, including elements such as:

- Identification of the risk,

- Description of the risk,

- Impact assessment (if it happens, what is impacted and how),

- Probability assessment (the likelihood of the risk actually materializing),

- Mitigation actions (what will be done if the risk materializes), and

- Responsibility (who is responsible for executing the mitigation actions).

6.2.4 Step 9: Identify the Required Data Sources

Throughout the project pilot, the project team is faced with a plethora of challenges, ranging from softer change

---

[31] Ibid, 127.

management issues to the perils of system integration. One of the risks of any ABPB Project is the identification and capture, from numerous sources across the organization, of financial and operational data (both empirical and judgmental) that are needed to build the Closed-Loop Model.

The Closed-Loop Model is a data intensive calculation of forecasted demand, consumption rates, current capacity, product revenue, and resource costs. The time and effort involved in identifying, documenting, and cataloging the data sources is imperative to enabling a sustainable and repeatable process. Consider the breadth of just some of the information required: labor supply and cost from human resources, supply and materiel costs from purchasing, product revenue from marketing and/or finance, forecasted unit requirements from sales, and operational capacity and consumption from operations. The extent of this information underscores the importance of using a cross-functional project team to leverage experience from across the organization.

Additional information about how to collect data and structure the information systems architecture is found in Chapter 11.

6.2.5 Step 10: Develop a Project Evaluation Plan

An evaluation plan determines how the project measures its own success. At what state can the project be considered successfully completed? Is success defined by realigning resources that would otherwise go under-utilized, thereby achieving greater capacity at no additional cost? Is it a fiscal period that executes with less overtime than would otherwise be necessary? Or is it simply creating the capability to re-assign resources quickly in response to changes in demand?

As part of the evaluation plan, a formal feedback loop, operating at pre-specified intervals, should be established so that project stakeholders can provide insight into the perceived successes and failures of the initiative. An interview or a survey halfway through the project to receive comments from stakeholders might be considered. A second interview or survey at the end of the project might also be informative.

This feedback and documentation becomes an important element in improving the implementation of later ABPB Projects, and refining the Closed-Loop Models. The results and lessons learned from one project become the input to successive projects within the ABPB Implementation Program. At a minimum, the assumptions of the Closed-Loop Model: demand estimates, consumption rates, capacity levels, operational balances, financial balances, and financial results should be documented and archived. Later project iterations can use the information about the variation between planned and actual results to improve consumption rates and assumptions.

Now that the tasks and actions necessary to Initiate and Plan each ABPB Project are understood, the book turns to a closer examination of the nuts and bolts of building the individual Closed-Loop Models.

7 CHAPTER

Developing the Initial Closed-Loop Model

Armed with an organizational approach to Initiating and Planning an ABPB Project, the next step involves developing the initial Closed-Loop Model and linking the initiative to the organization's long-term strategies.

7.1 DESIGNATING THE ORGANIZATION'S PLANNING PERIOD

Traditionally, organizations develop detailed operating and financial plans for the upcoming year and strategic plans for three to five years out, with the business environment generally being the guiding factor in determining the level of detail and the time horizon of both the short and long term plans. These plans are normally based on an analysis of historical costs as well as projected demands. But because most plans are based primarily on history, they often lack approaches to cope with the uncertainties of the future. The ABPB Process offers tools to help an organization build a Closed-Loop Model based on analyses of future demands, process improvements, product changes, and resource capacity. The ABPB Process also provides a framework for planning that can be much more dynamic than the more traditional fixed, yearly plan.

An important first step in designing a Closed-Loop Model is the decision as to what period the Closed-Loop Model should apply to and at what interim points, if any, progress should be reviewed and the Closed-Loop Model revised. Demand is rarely constant and often is affected by factors entirely out of an organization's control. The number and stability of factors that cause fluctuation in demand and availability of resources should be considered when deciding the most appropriate planning period for the organization.

Increasingly, organizations are choosing to forecast demand using a *rolling forecast* rather than a *static forecast*, ensuring that the demand for each planning period is based on the most current data and that the expectations are managed in a realistic fashion. While the ABPB Process is viable no matter what the forecast horizon, it works particularly well with a rolling forecast because the Closed-Loop Model focuses on prediction rather than historical analysis.

7.2 UNDERSTANDING THE BUILDING BLOCKS OF THE CLOSED-LOOP MODEL

Although there are significant differences between the implementation and application of Activity-Based Cost Management (ABCM) and Activity-Based Planning and Budgeting, there are similarities in the building blocks used to construct these types of systems. The existence of common building blocks in both systems will greatly assist in the initial implementation of a Closed-Loop Model, insofar as they provide, at a minimum, agreed-upon starting points for defining products/services, activities, and resources. (For additional information on the building blocks of any activity-based system, refer to Cokins 1996, Player and Keys 1996, or Stratton and McKinney 1999.) *Products/services* are what an organization delivers to its customers, and the *demand* for products and services is what leads to the consumption of *activities*. The definition of what constitutes a product or service is specific to each organization and situation, and will be included in the definition of the ABPB Process (and will often be common to or derived from an existing ABCM system).

If the Closed-Loop Model is completely focused on external customers, then the products/services are usually those things that customers pay for. Examples include:

- Manufacture and delivery of cars, trucks, SUVs, spare parts, and repair services for a car manufacturer,

- Delivery of legal services for a law firm, and

- Delivery of mail and packages (segregated by speed of delivery) for the postal services.

In internal situations, products/services may be defined as those provided by one part of the organization to another, irrespective of how the receiving unit pays for such items.

Examples include:

- A manufacturing plant makes components used at an assembly facility,

- A clerk processes weekly payroll to generate employees' paychecks, and

- A marketing employee prepares a brochure for use by the sales force.

And finally, there are unique definitions of products/services, along the lines discussed in Chapter 4; for example, the United States Department of Defense provides the *capability* necessary to defend and protect the United States.

The following sections explain the building blocks of the Closed-Loop Model, using Figure 7.1, the structure developed previously, for the reader's reference.

7.2.1 Demands for Products and Services

7.2.1.1 Demand Volumes

Once the definition of products/services has been agreed to and a complete listing generated, the organization must then estimate the *demand volume*, which is the quantity of demand for each defined product/service. Consumption of activities and resources is driven by this demand volume. Therefore, the need for consumption begins with a *demand*

Figure 7.1: The CAM-I ABPB Closed-Loop Model

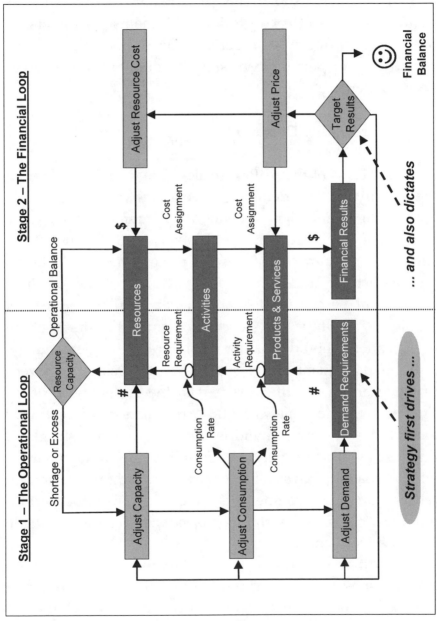

forecast for each product/service to be delivered. These demand forecasts should be specified in metrics such as number or units of each product, shipments, customers, or hours of a service by time period. Once specified, the time period should remain consistent throughout the Closed-Loop Model.

7.2.1.2 Forecasting Demand

The success of the ABPB Process is heavily dependent on the quality of the demand forecasts that are fed to it. Forecasting demand is dependent on many factors, some predictable or controllable and others that are not. For successful planning, the focus for forecasting should be on the predictable and controllable factors. Some of these factors will be specific to a particular industry or market segment, but there are several common factors that all organizations should consider when forecasting demand.

Demand quantities should be forecast for every product/service identified as part of the budgeting process. Trend or historical analysis, and extrapolations thereof, give a good idea of how demand is expected to grow, shrink, or fluctuate within the period. Coupling this trend analysis with a broader analysis of the market, including fact-finding related to new competitors and new product/service offerings, helps to determine projections of growth outside of the typical trends.

In addition to studying the market, the general economy and business climate should be reflected in demand forecasts. The extent to which such data is considered is largely determined by how demand for an organization's products/services fluctuates with broader economic performance. Also, growth in one area may lead to growth or decline in another; in economic terms, some products/services are complementary while others are substitutes. Additional details relating to demand forecasting are discussed in Chapter 10.

7.2.2 Activities Consumed by Demand

The demand for products/services results in the consumption of *activities*. Activities represent all work that an organization performs in the delivery of products/services. The activities required to deliver a product/service can be identified from a study of the processes that affect the delivery, again perhaps drawn from an existing ABCM system. Multiple activities are usually consumed by the demand for a single product/service, and while activities may consume other activities, ultimately, all activities must consume resources.

Examples of activities consumed by demand include the following (note that all of these examples are structured as verb-noun combinations):

- Enter claim,

- Debug software,

- Process order,

- Weld joint,

- Research case law,

- Repair production operator terminal,

- Supervise customer service representatives,

- Maintain aircraft,

- Call prospective customers, and

- Sell product/service.

Each product/service consumes a particular amount of each activity. To build the Closed-Loop Model, the *activity requirements* must be identified. Each activity requirement depends on the amount of demand for the product/service and the rate at which each demand consumes each activity. For an activity such as "sell product", the activity requirement could be the number of products to sell. For "weld joint" it would be the number of joints that require welding.

With the ABPB Process, multiple levels of activities should be defined, particularly in cases where consumption of an activity is based on characteristics that vary depending on the application of the activity to specific products/services. An activity such as "weld joint" may have three tasks (sub-activities): prepare to weld, weld, and verify whether the weld is properly done. The task of "verify whether the weld is properly done" could vary substantially in cost, depending on the type of product requiring a particular weld. For example, the amount of inspection of a weld in a refrigerator does not require the same rigor and documentation as a weld done for an aircraft.

As was shown in the call center example in Chapter 3, there are activities that are viewed as "business sustaining" and thus kept outside of the Closed-Loop Model. The costs of these activities are normally accounted for separately in assessing financial balance. Examples of business sustaining activities include:

- Develop human resource policy, and

- Perform strategic business planning.

7.2.3 Resources Consumed by Activities

Knowledge of what activities must be performed helps to define what resources are required to accomplish those activities. Resources are the economic elements that are consumed by activities and which cause organizations to incur cost. The definition of many resources may be drawn from an existing ABCM system. Examples of resources include people, materials, software licenses, supplies, equipment, facilities, and third party providers.

Resources can be classified into two principal categories. *Fixed resources* are those whose quantity is fixed within a specific time period and are paid for whether or not they are fully used.   Examples of fixed resources include full-time employees, facilities, and equipment.   *Variable resources* are those that are consumed and paid for as needed.   Examples of variable resources include contract labor, consumable supplies, most forms of basic utilities, and certain software licenses.

7.2.4 Differentiating Between Activities and Services

When building a Closed-Loop Model, there can be confusion between the definition of a service and an activity. This confusion happens when the service is provided directly through an activity and the service thus cannot be distinguished from the activity. For example, a bank teller is providing *services* to clients, such as cashing checks, accepting deposits, and providing account balances. However, these services are also the *activities* that the teller must perform to deliver the services. These situations can be modeled either as specific services being delivered or as the activities that fall under a more generic label such as "customer service."   A decision as to which is more appropriate should be based on the specific goals of the organization and the particular application of the Closed-Loop Model.

When identifying activities, an organization should garner input from all units and functions that contribute to the delivery of each product/service. After all the activities and resources have been identified, then expert knowledge and common sense can be used to combine them into classifications or groupings that are sensible and manageable.

7.3 MODELING AT THE RIGHT LEVEL OF DETAIL

Once the building blocks are understood, the organization is ready to determine the best way to use them to develop a value-added Closed-Loop Model. When developing the Closed-Loop Model, the organization should start with an understanding of the appropriate level of detail required. A successful Closed-Loop Model has activities and resources grouped to a level of detail that aligns with the data available, but not at so detailed a level that the analysis and use of the Closed-Loop Model becomes impractical.

The project team tasked with building a Closed-Loop Model should decide if the incremental effort of developing a more detailed model that, for example, tracks production line activities to the level of fastening each nut and bolt is of sufficient value, or if a simpler model that tracks assembling specific subsystems or even entire systems is more appropriate. A very detailed model could inundate the modeling team with more data than they could possibly process or deal with in a meaningful and timely fashion, thereby increasing the chances of failure of the entire initiative.

Before an organization can effectively build a Closed-Loop Model, time and effort should be applied to defining a level of detail for activities and resources that is both possible and achievable. A level of detail is possible if there is historical data or organizational knowledge available that supports analysis at that level.　The level of detail is achievable if can be accomplished with the amount of resources and within the scheduled time allocated to building the Closed-Loop Model.

7.4　CONNECTING THE BUILDING BLOCKS – CONSUMPTION RATES, DRIVERS, AND METRICS

Having used the building blocks (demands, activities, and resources) to identify and group the activities and resources consumed in the organization, the next step is to construct the model of how these activities and resources are consumed by the organization's products and services.　The model:

- Shows the flow of activity and resource consumption and relates this flow to demand for specific products and services, and

- Sets the stage for the identification of drivers and the application of consumption rate relationships.

7.4.1　Determining Activity Drivers, Resource Drivers, and Consumption Rates

While in aggregate all products and services consume all activities (other than business sustaining ones), each product or service likely consumes each given activity at a unique rate.　The rate at which a specific unit of demand consumes an activity is referred to as the activity consumption rate. The *activity requirement* is the number of occurrences of a single activity required to meet the total quantity of demand, and is therefore a function of both the demand volume and the activity consumption rate.   Factors unique to each product and service are used to determine *how* its particular demand consumes an activity. These factors are referred to as *activity drivers*.

For example, consider a factory that produces an automobile bumper composed of multiple pieces. Demand has been estimated at 1,000,000 type A bumpers for the next budgeting period. One of the activities required to produce a single bumper is "weld joint", where the activity requirement is expressed as the number of joints that require welding. As each type A bumper has five joints that require welding, the consumption rate for the "weld joint" activity is 5.   Therefore, the activity requirement is 5,000,000 (the consumption rate of 5 multiplied by the total number of bumpers needed, which is 1,000,000). In this example, the type of bumper is an activity driver that determines the consumption rate for the activity.

Each activity requires a specific amount of each resource that it consumes. This resource requirement is a function of both the activity requirement and the resource consumption rate. The resource consumption rate refers to the amount of a resource that is consumed by a single occurrence of an activity. Factors unique to each activity determine the rate at which it consumes specific resources.   These factors are referred to as *resource drivers*.

Continuing with the bumper example, suppose that the "weld joint" activity consumes the "welder" resource. On average, it takes the welder five minutes to weld a joint; this is the resource consumption rate. Given an activity requirement of 5,000,000, with a consumption rate of 5 minutes per activity unit, the resource requirement for the welder for the "weld joint" activity is 416,667 hours (5,000,000 x 5 = 25,000,000 minutes / 60 minutes per hour = 416,667 hours).

If there were more than one skill level of welder, such as experienced and novice, where one level was more efficient at welding than the other, this skill level information could be a driver that would determine the correct consumption rate of the welder resource based on the "weld joint" activity. Alternatively, the organization could direct the "weld joint" activity on a product-specific basis, such that there would be a unique activity established for each product; this approach, however, is fairly rare.

The identification of drivers and the determination of consumption rates can be complicated. Identifying drivers and consumption rates requires collecting and analyzing historical data, assessing planned product/service and process changes, as well as understanding the building blocks used in the Closed-Loop Model and how those building blocks interact.

7.4.2 Determining Consumption Measures

There are several different ways in which consumption for an activity or resource can be measured:

- **Unit measures** – each output consumes a specific volume of input (a single or average call consumes 5.25 minutes of technician time). [32]

- **Batch measures** – a batch of output consumes a unit of input (the setup for a production run of any size requires 30 minutes of an operator's time).

- **Ratio measures** – a ratio is used to determine how multiple inputs are consumed by a single output (the resources used to make a bumper consist of 60 percent full-time and 40 percent part-time labor).

- **Constant measures** – input is consumed at a single rate regardless of output volume (a parking lot requires a single attendant).

- **Allocation measures** – input is consumed through allocation without regard to output volume (an executive's salary is allocated on the basis of number of organizational units).

---

[32] Although each of these measures is described with a single number, in practice the number should be taken to mean a narrow range. For example, a single call may take anywhere from 5.0 – 5.5 minutes per call, a range narrow enough that a single point estimate can be used. Similar examples can be developed for the other types of measures.

The *consumption measures* used for each Closed-Loop Model depend on the types of activities and resources being consumed. The different ways that consumption occurs in a Closed-Loop Model should be considered to develop appropriate consumption rates.

7.5 ESTIMATING CONSUMPTION RATES AND DRIVERS

7.5.1 Collecting Historical Data and Performing Regression Analysis

Estimating consumption rates is a critical aspect of building an accurate Closed-Loop Model, since it is through consumption rates that future requirements for activities and resources can be predicted.   In the simplest case, a consumption rate can be estimated by evaluating historical data to determine how a resource has been consumed by an activity, and then projecting that rate to future periods. However, the simplest case may not be the best.   By performing a more thorough analysis of historical information, several key drivers can be identified and consumption rates can be estimated based on the relationship of the key drivers to actual consumption.

Consider the example of an information technology (IT) shared services function. One of the typical activities of such a function is "respond to trouble calls".   For every workstation deployed, historical analysis has indicated that there is an average of 4.6 trouble calls per year and the average trouble call takes 5.4 hours of an IT technician's time to resolve. Thus, the activity consumption rate would be 4.6 calls per workstation per year, and the resource consumption rate would be 5.4 hours per trouble call. Given a particular demand for workstations supported, n, the activity requirement can be estimated at (n x 4.6), and the resource requirement at [(n x 4.6) x 5.4]. This example illustrates how future period activity and resource requirements can be estimated merely through the application of historical consumption rates.

Suppose, however, a more detailed analysis of this data indicates that although the *average* time for a technician to resolve a problem is 5.4 hours, more than 80 percent of the trouble calls actually require less than 0.5 hours to resolve, while a very small number of calls take more than 20 hours to resolve. This data indicates that a simple average may not result in the most accurate resource consumption rate. After further analysis to determine exactly what differentiates the 0.5 hour trouble calls from the 20+ hour service calls, it becomes clear that trouble calls can be classified into two categories: complex and simple. Thus, the complexity classification is a resource driver.

Additionally, the data shows that novice computer users and new employees generate twice as many trouble calls as more experienced computer users, leading to the conclusion that the level of user experience is an activity driver. A mathematical analysis of the activity drivers, such as a regression analysis, should result in a relationship that describes how the resource consumption rate changes with the complexity of the problem and how the activity consumption rate changes with the experience of the user.

This kind of analysis can be repeated *ad nauseum* since there are usually a very large number of factors that impact consumption of a particular resource or activity. In order to reduce the time spent on the analysis, it is important to understand that many of these factors either have minimal impact or are close to impossible to predict in the early planning stages. Therefore, users should seek to identify and then focus on the few factors that are predictable and provide the most value at the least possible cost.

7.5.2 Finding Relationships Using Analogous Data

While an analysis of historical cost, technical, and performance data is often the most appropriate way to identify drivers and estimate consumption rates, sometimes that historical data is unavailable or has not been tracked in a way that makes it usable for analysis. In such cases, analogy is another method that might be applied. Analogy allows the data pertaining to an existing product/service, activity, or resource to be used to estimate or project the drivers and consumption rates for a new and similar product/service, activity, or resource. For example, a company that is launching a new line of bumpers may use the consumption rates and drivers of an existing bumper with similar characteristics to estimate the metrics for the new bumper. This method is most successful when more than one analogy exists and the information can be blended or averaged (mathematically or judgmentally) in a way that makes sense. Further, organizations can use judgment to make changes to analogous data to better reflect quantifiable differences between existing and new items.

7.5.3 Using Expert Knowledge

In the absence of analogous or historical data, business planners and budgeters can draw upon organizational intelligence. Experienced and knowledgeable individuals (often referred to as Subject Matter Experts or SMEs) within an organization can provide insights into how things get done and how much or what it takes to get them done. Soliciting information from a cross-section of such individuals, combining the results of their expertise, and removing outliers should result in a fairly good estimate of what factors drive consumption and at what rates.

Polling of experts within the organization should be done through a consistent and formal process where each expert is given the same set of stimuli, questions, and assumptions. This process ensures that the opinions are all within the same context. One technique for polling an organization's SMEs is the *Delphi method*, a formalized process for extracting "data" from such experts. Ideally, the experts are brought together and briefed on the purpose of the data collection to ensure common context. Each expert is then taken through a series of questions intended to extract his/her expert opinion on a particular subject; this questioning process may be performed as a group or individually to avoid having the meeting dominated by one person. The "educated guesses" from the experts are then combined and analyzed to form an "expert" opinion on the subject.

The Delphi approach of drawing on the views of multiple "experts" avoids the inevitable human bias that occurs when a single expert is consulted. Having multiple "experts" provide opinions balances out individual biases.[33]

7.5.4 Combining Methods

To develop the best Closed-Loop Model possible within reasonable constraints, some combination of data collection and regression analysis, analogy, expert opinion, research, and common sense should be applied. Combining methods is appealing and beneficial because the methods tend to complement each other and can help identify breakdowns in any one method of the data gathering process.

No single method, or even combination of methods, used to identify drivers and estimate consumption rates will give precisely the "right" predictions. No matter how well researched and verified, the prediction is still an estimate. The predictions generated by a Closed-Loop Model should be verified with the actual consumption rates and expenditures that occur in each period in order to figure out which drivers and consumption rates are appropriate and which estimates are accurate. This verification enables continual refinement and calibration (Chapter 9 contains further details on updating the Closed-Loop Model).

---

[33] On the other hand, averaging will dilute the impact of a particularly "gifted" expert who has exceptional insight.

7.6 DEFINING RESOURCE CAPACITIES

Capacity describes how many units of a resource are available for consumption within a specific time period. Only resources have capacity;[34] activities consume capacity.[35] Each resource has a limited amount of capacity that can be consumed. People only work so many hours a day, properly skilled temporary help may be unavailable, equipment has scheduled and unscheduled maintenance and downtimes, material and supplies sometimes are limited in availability, and facility space is limited by the square footage available. Although the idea of capacity is fairly simple, understanding capacity can be complex.

7.6.1 Understanding Fixed and Variable Resources

Since some resources are consumed in the same units as they are available or acquired and some are not, resource capacity and consumption are measured in both *availability units* and *consumption units*. Human resources are generally available as FTEs but their time is actually consumed in hours. On the other hand, supplies are generally consumed in the units they are available (for example, safety shoes and

---

[34] It can also be argued that activities and processes have capacity. At one level this is true, but ultimately activity and process capacity is provided by resources.

[35] In some cases, resources cause the consumption of other resources, but even this consumption is caused by the performance of an activity somewhere in the organization.

safety glasses for production line staff[36]). There are three ways to describe resource capacity in relation to the way resources are consumed:

- **Variable** – the resource is available in the same units that it is consumed (for example, safety shoes and safety glasses).

- **Step Fixed** – Resources are available in constant quantity over specific periods of time, but an increase in demand for consumption units of a resource eventually requires a step increase in availability units. For example, if an employee can work 1,500 hours in a year and substantially more than that is required, then two staff must be hired if overtime, temporary labor, and contract labor are excluded or consumed to capacity. Another example pertains to flight attendants: for safety reasons, a minimum of one attendant is required on a flight and an additional attendant is required for every, say, 30 passengers; thus, as soon as 31 passengers are booked, a second flight attendant is required; at 61 passengers, a third is required, and so on.

- **Fixed** – A constant quantity of a resource is on hand regardless of how many consumption units are

---

[36] This ignores the fact that although many supplies are delivered in bulk, the purchase price of these items is still expressed in the unit of consumption. For example, while safety shoes may be acquired in hundreds, the price is likely to be on a per pair basis.

required. This definition applies over what is often termed a "reasonable range" meaning that the quantity available is fixed provided that the requirement stays within the normal bounds of a business cycle. Facility space is a prime example, where the space owned or leased is, say, 100,000 square feet and can not readily change whether 90,000 or 110,000 are actually needed in different periods. However, if 200,000 square feet were needed over a sustained period of time, clearly the existing availability would need to be supplemented; and conversely, if only 40,000 square feet was needed in the long run, the organization should seek to sell, sub-lease, or otherwise reduce its space consumption. Another way of looking at this is that "fixed" quantities are simply those with very large and infrequent steps.

Most resources are variable in the long term, but fixed in the short term. In the long run, staff can be re-assigned, terminated, or hired. New machines can be purchased or sold. Organizations can move to bigger plants or smaller office space as the need for space changes. A successful Closed-Loop Model should consider the impacts that the time dimension has on planning and should look at capacity as it changes annually, quarterly, monthly, with the seasons, and with economic and technological conditions of the marketplace.

7.6.2 Understanding the Costs and Implications of Unused Capacity

A Closed-Loop Model can identify how and when resources are consumed by demands for products and services. Because the quantity available of most resources is fixed in the short term, there are times when certain resources are at least partially idle or under-utilized (meaning that they are being operated at less than the maximum rate, such as a soft drink production line running at 1,000 cans/minute when its rated speed is 1,200 cans/minute). However, an organization generally needs to keep the resources that are required to meet average demands and, in many cases, to at least meet some share of peak or seasonal demands. Maintaining this *buffer capacity* must be accounted for in an organization's planning. The ABPB Process and Closed-Loop Model allow an organization to forecast unused capacity and thus provide the opportunity to reduce unused capacity by shifting resources or re-scheduling activities. Although the intent of a Closed-Loop Model is to determine the best plan for meeting specific demands for products and services, the cost of unused capacity should also be included in the analysis. A more complete discussion of capacity is in Chapter 8.

7.7 IDENTIFYING INTERNAL INCREASES TO DEMAND

Not all applications of the ABPB Process relate directly to external products and services. At times, the resource requirements generated by the need for a product or service can create demand for products and services within the organization itself.

Consider an organization that sells clothing through catalog sales. As the demand for clothing increases, the requirement for telephone operators increases. However, each new hire also increases the demand for central services because each new operator needs to be set up with a workstation, needs training on using that workstation, and requires ongoing support when there is a problem or question. Such situations are not unique to catalog sales but occur in every organization's internal or contracted support functions. This situation is discussed in greater detail in Chapter 10, Section 10.3, entitled "Understanding Complex Activity Interactions".

Some planning and budgeting systems are internally focused rather than externally focused. An organization may need to model services that are delivered internally as well as those that go to external customers, although ultimately all demands need to be driven by the demand for external products and services. Some organizations use this type of internal modeling to identify areas for outsourcing or process improvement. Examples of internal services likely to be targeted for this type of planning and budgeting include central services, such as information technology and human resources.

7.8 SUMMARY

This chapter has identified the key building blocks needed to develop an initial Closed-Loop Model. Building a Closed-Loop Model is a big step in executing the ABPB Process within an organization, but it is only the beginning. Once the building blocks have been identified and the connections made, the organization should compare actual against predicted results to learn where assumptions are incorrect and where refinement is necessary. In addition, the organization needs to develop the processes and procedures needed to update and sustain the Closed-Loop Model over time.

The next chapter provides advice on how to analyze data and manage using the Closed-Loop Model.

8 CHAPTER

Using the Closed-Loop Model to Manage the Business

Once the Closed-Loop Model is in place, the plan's value comes from its use in managing the business: focusing attention on the most important items to adjust and control. In all organizations, there are more opportunities to manage and improve than there are time and resources to take advantage of them. The key is to use the plan to determine what, when, where, and how to manage. The plan generated by the Closed-Loop Model can provide a rational method of making choices.

Traditional budgeting approaches compare actual results to a fixed budget, usually on a general ledger line item basis, assuming that the budget is an internal benchmark that can be used to evaluate operations. In contrast, the budget derived from the Closed-Loop Model can be measured against specific operational metrics to provide a more effective benchmark. Moreover, because the Closed-Loop Model incorporates a wealth of operational linkages and can be updated or adjusted automatically and rapidly, it provides a dynamic benchmark, updating the key assumptions and analyzing the impact of changes to those values.

The Closed-Loop Model provides a way to sort and evaluate issues because the underlying operational relationships drive the financial results. Using the financial and operational information together enables management to categorize and rank the various issues and resolve the most critical ones. Furthermore, because financial results are usually driven from underlying operational relationships, changes may be specifically targeted for maximum impact to the bottom line or any other key financial metric.

All plans require assumptions, and in some cases pure guesses, concerning future activities and results. The Closed-Loop Model organizes these assumptions into detailed cause and effect relationships, each of which is expressed mathematically. As the results predicted by the Closed-Loop Model are compared to actual results, management asks the what, when, where, why, and how questions. In so doing, management evaluates, understands, and refines assumptions and can also investigate operations that are not performing as expected. Over time, management can debug the initial model assumptions, and identify which areas of the organization are changing. In addition, the analysis points out what was unexpected or unplanned and guides management toward the changes that need to be made in the next update of the Closed-Loop Model.

Most organizations' plans and budgets have countless assumptions and relationships, most of which are often not documented or even made explicit. The Closed-Loop Model groups the list of key assumptions into five areas, referred to as "Control Levers":

Operational Levers	Lever 1, Demand Quantities
	Lever 2, Consumption Rates
	Lever 3, Resource Capacities
Financial Levers	Lever 4, Resource Unit Costs
	Lever 5, Product/Service Prices

It is through changes to one or more of these five levers that management can drive results. Understanding them is therefore essential for management to be able to drive *desired* change rather than simply reacting to events. These levers, sequenced to understand the organization's results,[37] are highlighted in Figure 8.1.

The list of levers overlaps extensively with the levers from a traditional budget plan.[38] However, there are four distinct reasons why the plan generated from the Closed-Loop Model will be more successful:

---

[37] Analyzing the budget is different from preparing the budget. Therefore, the sequence used in building the budget in Chapters 2 and 3 is different from the one used in analyzing the budget in this chapter.

[38] Traditional budgeting approaches contain three of these levers: Lever 1, demand quantities; Lever 4, resource unit costs; and Lever 5, product/service prices. Traditional budgeting approaches do not contain Lever 2, activity and resource consumption rates. Lever 3, resource capacities, is partially reflected in traditional models since resource supply may be included, but it is rarely explicitly matched against the quantity demanded of each resource.

Figure 8.1: The Five Levers of the CAM-I ABPB Closed-Loop Model

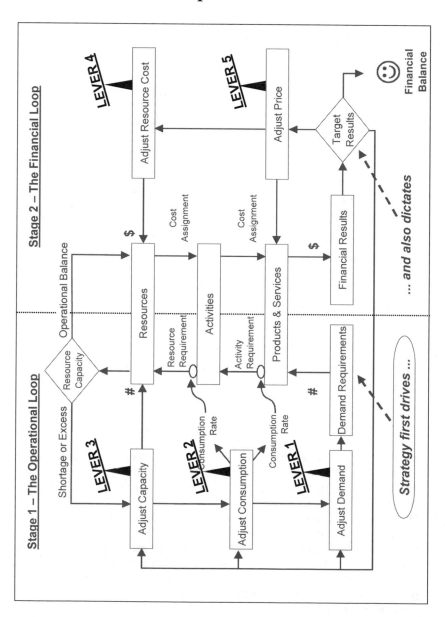

1. The Closed-Loop Model is built on cause-and-effect relationships and is based on a "real" model of how the organization's inputs relate to its outputs.

2. The level of detail available from the Closed-Loop Model is more granular than in most traditional planning and budgeting approaches.

3. The activity and resource consumption rates are explicit in the Closed-Loop Model whereas they are not used in most traditional approaches.

4. The inherent cross-functional view in the Closed-Loop Model enables the organization to track down problems that cross organizational boundaries, as each unit's models are integrated across the organization. (For more detail, see "Understanding Complex Activity Interactions" in Chapter 10.)

Analyzing the differences between actual results and planned results lets organizations determine the degree of accuracy of each model assumption. It also identifies areas where process performance may differ from what was expected.

The following sections examine each of the five Control Levers in greater detail.   The call center application presented in Chapter 3 is extended here to discuss the effect of changing each of these levers.   In these analyses, the approved operating plan - the base year results as shown in Chapter 3 - of the call center will be shown (Figure 8.2) followed by an example of actual operating performance and financial results (Figure 8.3). The differences between Figures 8.2 and 8.3 reflect all of the variances in demand, consumption rates, resource capacities, resource unit costs, and service prices that the call center experienced as compared to its plan, and the consequent financial results.

These analyses are presented in a historical structure, so that management can understand and assess the impact of changes to each lever individually and cumulatively. A parallel approach can be used to generate "what-if" scenarios, in other words, applying the Closed-Loop Model as a planning tool.

Sections 8.1 through 8.5 of this chapter then analyze the impact of the variance for each individual lever, but in a manner that builds towards the actual total financial results. Thus, Section 8.1 analyzes the impact of the change in demand volume, holding all other levers constant. Section 8.2 analyzes the impact of the variances in consumption rates, adding to the impact of the new demand level, but holding the remaining three levers unchanged, and so on. Once the impact of the variance in the final lever - service prices - is analyzed, the organization will be in a position to understand the impact of each individual lever as well as the inter-action between the levers.

The approved plan of the call center (the base year results) is shown in Figure 8.2. As one would expect, there were significant differences between planned results and actual results generated for this example, shown in Figure 8.3.

Figure 8.2: The Approved Plan From the Call Center Example, Base Year

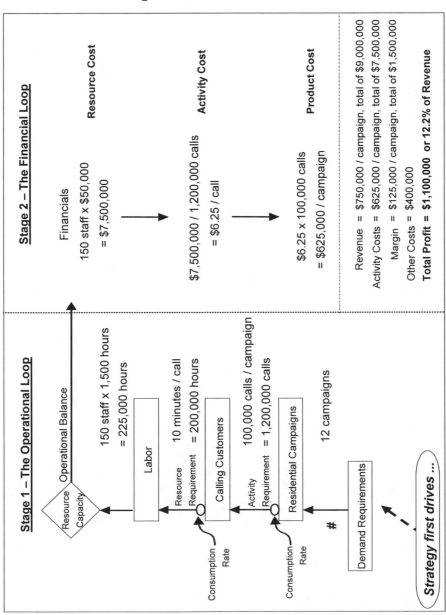

Figure 8.3: The Combined Effect of Changing All Five Levers

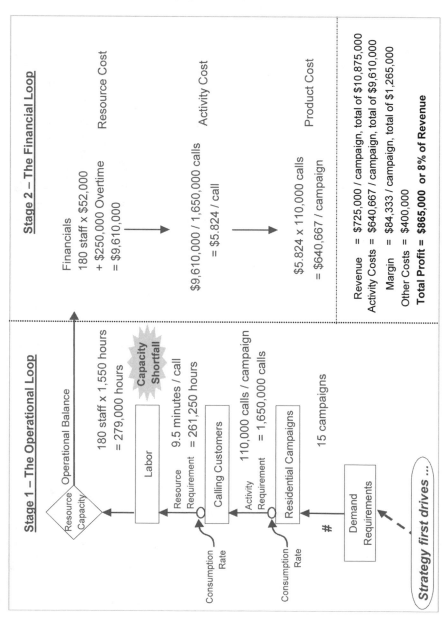

In most organizations using traditional approaches, the only information available would be the financial results box on the lower right-hand side of Figure 8.3.   Certainly the sales function would be aware of the variance in demand volumes; the call center's operations managers would know the details of the variances in consumption rates and the increase in resource capacity; human resources would be familiar with the rationale for the higher resource unit costs; and sales and/or marketing would have full knowledge of the reduction in service prices.   However, without an integrated Closed-Loop Model, none of the managers in the call center would have knowledge of all of these variances, and hence explaining the variance in the financial results is extremely difficult and unlikely to be accurate.[39]   Analyzing the impact of the variance of each individual lever is the purpose of each of the five sections that follow.

8.1 LEVER 1 - DEMAND QUANTITIES

Because demand quantities are the starting point of the Closed-Loop Model, they are also the logical starting point of any analysis of differences between budget and actual results.   Questions that might be asked include: What is the impact of the difference between the actual demand

---

[39] Most readers are familiar with the contortions in language and logic used by controllers and other managers to explain the reasons for variances in performance. Without the linkage between operating and financial metrics, as provided in the Closed-Loop Model, explanations such as "Revenues were lower because customers bought less volume than what was expected in the plan" (this is a real explanation!) will remain all too common.

experienced and the volume that was planned? What about the mix? Although the absolute demand level is monitored in most organizations, the Closed-Loop Model permits a *product-specific* examination of the impact of changes in demand on actual operations.

Using the Closed-Loop Model, the impact of the actual demand of 15 promotional campaigns instead of the planned 12 campaigns can be estimated. Figure 8.4 indicates the Closed-Loop Model reflecting solely that change. The increase in demand generated $2.25 million in additional revenues ($11,250,000 versus the base year amount of $9,000,000), but also – initially - leaves the center without an Operational Balance.

How so? In this simple case, a capacity shortfall occurred: 150 employees were not sufficient to handle the volume of calls that they were required to make. In order to retain operational balance, the simplest change to make was the hiring of 30 additional staff while maintaining a level of buffer capacity similar to the base year, thus boosting the staff complement from 150 in Figure 8.2 to 180 in Figure 8.4. The cost of this decision was $1,500,000 (30 staff at $50,000 each). The actual profit earned from these 15 campaigns reflected the cost of hiring 30 additional staff, and was therefore $1,850,000.

Organizations can use the demand quantity lever to address significant questions, such as:

- What resource capacity requirements would the Closed-Loop Model have calculated if actual demand had been known?

Figure 8.4: Impact of Actual Demand

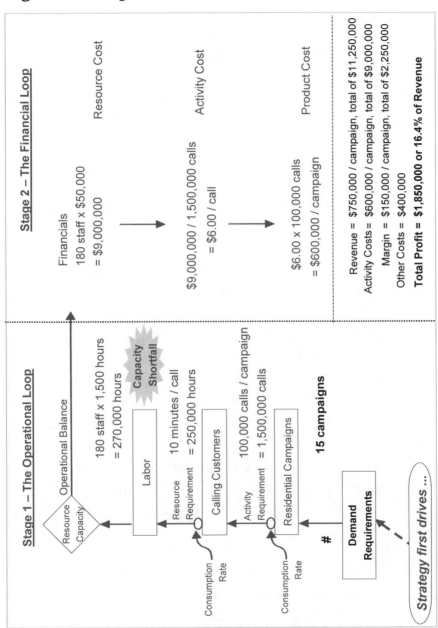

- What would have been the level of profitability if actual demand had been known?

  o By product, product family, product line;

  o By customer, customer group, customer type; and

  o By channel.

- What would have been the total resource costs if actual demand had been known?

- How have the organization's processes performed with this level of demand?

- Were resource capacity levels adequate?

- Did demand come from unexpected sources, i.e. were activities undertaken due to new products or customers?

- How did the demand mix stress the organization's processes, i.e. did the unexpected demand mix materially change the quantity of each activity performed?

Analysis with the Closed-Loop Model goes beyond traditional demand analysis by examining the impact of actual demand on activities and resources. Managers can ask the question: If actual demand had been known, what would have been the necessary resources?

8.2 LEVER 2 – CONSUMPTION RATES

Following the flow of the Closed-Loop Model, the next lever to examine is the impact of consumption rates. Consumption rates link demand requirements to resource requirements. As discussed in Chapter 7, the Closed-Loop Model has two types of such rates: activity consumption rates and resource consumption rates.[40]

Continuing with the situation in Section 8.1, the actual demand of 15 campaigns and the resulting increase in resource capacity to 180 staff are retained. The changes made in this section are that the activity consumption rate was 110,000 instead of 100,000 calls per campaign, and that the resource consumption rate dropped from 10 minutes to 9.5 minutes per call. The combined effect of these two changes is shown in Figure 8.5.

The increase in demand and the increase in the activity consumption rate had the effect of increasing the activity and resource requirement quite substantially. However, the increase in the resource requirement was partially offset by the improvement in the resource consumption rate. The

---

[40] Resource consumption rates and activity consumption rates in any Closed-Loop Model are just part of the picture. In a real system, resources, activities, and cost objects will be linked across processes and, potentially, across organizational units. Examining the network of links is of great value in managing variances across the entire network. See "Understanding Complex Activity Interactions" in Chapter 10 for further discussion.

Figure 8.5: Incremental Impact of Actual
Consumption Rates

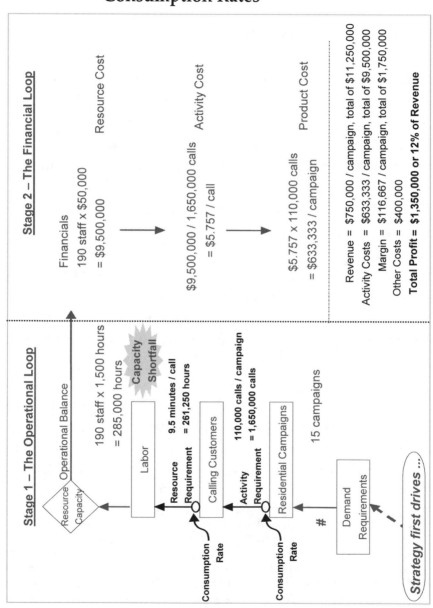

net effect was that the demand-caused increase in staffing levels – as discussed in Section 8.1 – was insufficient to handle the required number of calling hours (the resource requirement) plus a fairly stable level of buffer capacity:

- Planned resource requirement = 200,000 hours + 25,000 hours of buffer, met with 150 staff, and

- Resource requirement due to change in demand = 250,000 + 20,000 hours of buffer, met with 180 staff.

The resource requirement due to the changes in consumption rates and demand equals 261,250 hours + 23,750 hours of buffer, was met with 190 staff. In other words, to meet the increased resource requirement, the organization was forced to hire ten additional people at a cost of $500,000. Combining the results of changes to the first and second levers of the Closed-Loop Model shows that profits fell to $1,350,000. This calculation is also shown in Figure 8.5.

It is worth noting that the impact of each lever can still be seen in isolation. The simple effect of increased demand and increased staffing levels resulted in profits of $1,850,000 (Figure 8.4) versus the plan of $1,100,000 (Figure 8.2). But the effect of the changes in consumption rates and the additional resource requirements imposed by those changes results in profits declining to $1,350,000 (Figure 8.5). In other words, the change in consumption rates and the resulting small increase in resources required cost the call center $500,000.

The consumption rate lever can be used to examine important questions such as:

- What consumption rates were actually experienced for activities?

- What consumption rates were actually experienced for resources?

- If demand was much higher and resource capacity remained as planned, how did the organization's processes perform?

  - If a better consumption rate was experienced, how can the organization make that improvement a permanent part of its planning and its operations?

  - Was the organization able to better utilize slack (i.e. excess or buffer) resources?

- If demand was much lower, how did the process perform?

  - Is a higher consumption rate simply wasting resources?

  - Did the organization use slack and/or excess capacity for training and development?

o   Did special projects absorb the excess capacity? Were the projects economically justified?

- Did the process maintain required measures for quality and cycle time, as well as the consumption rates?[41]

- What process improvements need to be implemented? What impact will they have?

- How did the change in consumption rates change the profitability of products and customers?

8.3 LEVER 3 - RESOURCE CAPACITY

The third operations lever is resource capacity. Once demand and the two consumption rates are known, and activity requirements calculated, the two key measures for each resource are how many resource units are needed and the unit capacity of each resource. The more challenging of these measures is the unit capacity of each resource, particularly when one is dealing with human resources. Since equipment is engineered and generally more specialized, its capacity (both in terms of quantity and what it can be used to do) is generally known and has defined

---

[41] A dynamic interrelationship exists between consumption rates, quality, and cycle time assumptions. The Closed-Loop Model generally assumes constant quality and cycle time measures. However, as these important measures vary and the organization makes changes to maintain say, the quality level, the impact on the consumption rate must be assessed.

limits.[42] However, human resources are not engineered, can perform a variety of tasks, and are more self-directed. Therefore, comparing the plan to actual results can generate insights and questions about the capacity of all types of resources and especially personnel.

Figure 8.6 continues extending the call center example, retaining the changes from the previous sections. It shows that the organization was able to do the required work with only 180 employees. How was this possible? By having each employee work about 50 hours of overtime, resulting in an additional cost of $250,000. Also, the initial planning assumed that 25,000 hours would be required as a buffer capacity. However, actual resources supplied only allowed for 17,750 of these hours. The net effect is that profits improved due to having slightly fewer employees and utilizing less buffer capacity. These gains were partially offset by the additional cost of overtime.

The net effect of adding the third lever to the previous two is that there is a $250,000 decline in cost and of course a parallel increase in profit. In other words, the net effect of substituting 50 hours of overtime per FTE in lieu of hiring 10 additional FTEs, plus reducing the level of buffer capacity, is a profit improvement of $250,000. Whether this gain is sufficient to accept the increased risk due to having less

---

[42] Most equipment is acquired for a specific purpose or purposes, with maximum and recommended operating metrics from the manufacturer. Machines likely have maximum speeds (often both an absolute maximum as well as a lower maximum speed for sustained use) and recommended maintenance programs.

Figure 8.6: Incremental Impact of Actual Resource Capacity

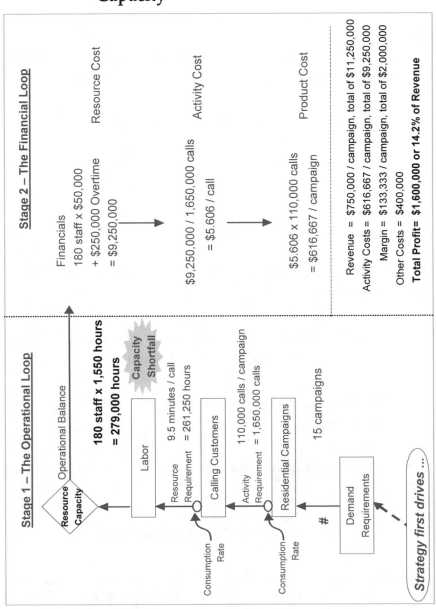

buffer capacity is a judgment question for management.[43] Therefore, when the actual demands, consumption rates, and capacity are considered, the profit earned was $1,600,000.

Organizations can use the resource capacity lever to address questions such as:

- What is the true capacity of personnel?

- How does actual equipment utilization compare to planned utilization?

- Where are there significant resource shortfalls?

- Is there surplus capacity that can be deployed? Where is it?

- What are the cross-training possibilities for personnel to assist in relieving capacity shortfalls?

- Are personnel working excessive overtime to meet requirements?

- What job improvements are necessary to better match people to jobs?

- What process improvements are needed?

---

[43] CAM-I's recommendation is to include the cost of nominal amounts of buffer capacity in product or service cost, rather than as a separate expense charge (Klammer 1996, 72).

- How did the change in capacity change the profitability of products and customers?

The Closed-Loop Model enables analyses of capacity utilization at the level of each modeled resource rather than at the department level available in traditional approaches (if at all). Beyond the immediate value of this type of analysis, an organization can drive further to obtain a deeper understanding of the "true" capacity of its personnel.

Another opportunity is to integrate this resource analysis with the CAM-I Capacity Model (Klammer 1996). The Capacity Model identifies the three major categories of capacity: Productive, Non-productive, and Idle. The Capacity Model also provides flexible classifications of the major categories as noted in Table 8.7.

Based on the capacity states defined by the Capacity Model, the organization can create a *Capacity Time Template*. This template analyzes time by its various states. The benchmark in the Capacity Model is that time is measured on a 24 hour per day, 365 days per year basis, for a total of 8,760 hours. This benchmark forces the organization to recognize how *all time* is being used, not just the typical daily eight hours of "working" time. Equipment and facilities could theoretically be used day and night but management policies or other factors may not enable them to be used on that basis. The Capacity Model forces the explicit recognition of all of these limitations. Human resources cannot work day and night as they have higher maintenance

Table 8.7: The CAM-I Capacity Model

Rated Capacity	Summary Model	Industry Specific Model	Strategy Specific Model
Rated Capacity	Idle	Not Marketable	Excess Not Usable
		Off Limits	Management Policy
			Contractual
			Legal
		Marketable	Idle But Usable
	Non-productive	Standby	Process Balance
			Variability
		Waste	Scrap
			Rework
			Yield Loss
		Maintenance	Scheduled
			Unscheduled
		Set-Ups	Time
			Volume
			Change-Over
	Productive	Process Development	
		Product Development	
		Good Products	

Source: Klammer 1996

requirements than equipment. Therefore, a significant portion of each employee's capacity is used for nights and weekends. However, it is very useful and informative to analyze people capacity on a similar basis as equipment or facilities. Table 8.8 provides a typical Capacity Time Template for a call center operator.

Overlaying the Capacity Time Template with costs appropriate to each of the various capacity states creates an

Table 8.8: The CAM-I Capacity Model - Time Template for Human Resources

Rated Capacity	Summary Model	Industry Specific Model		Strategy Specific Model	
Rated Capacity 8,760	Idle 6,485	Not Marketable	5,790	Nights & Weekends	5,790
		Off Limits	176	Vacation	80
				Holidays	96
		Marketable	519	Overtime	50
				Scheduling	469
	Non-Productive 775	Standby	300	Variability	300
		Maintenance	475	Training	100
				General Meetings	50
				Breaks	50
				Other Downtime	275
	Productive 1,500	Making Calls	1,500		

Source: Adapted from Klammer 1996

Economic Template.[44]   Because human resources are generally not paid for nights and weekends, these capacity states have no cost. However, overtime often has an additional cost.

---

[44] The employees' paid base hours consist of the sum of productive plus nonproductive plus off limits plus scheduling hours, a total of 2,920 hours (see Table 8.8).   The wage rate therefore works out to $52,000/2920 hours = $17.81 per hour.   This rate can be used to calculate the cost of each capacity state in Table 8.9, except for overtime. The overtime rate is $250,000 / (180 FTE * 50 hours/FTE) = $27.78 per hour.

Table 8.9 demonstrates a typical Economic Template for operators such as those in the call center example, using the final resource costs from Figure 8.3.

Integrating the Closed-Loop Model and the Capacity Model provides insights into how capacity was used and its cost, and provides valuable information to management.

Table 8.9: The CAM-I Capacity Model - Economic Template for Human Resources

Rated Capacity	Summary Model	Industry Specific Model		Strategy Specific Model	
	Idle $12,875	Not Marketable		Nights & Weekends	
		Off Limits	$3,134	Vacation	$1,425
				Holidays	$1,710
		Marketable	$9,741	Overtime	$1,389
				Scheduling	$8,352
Rated Capacity ($52,000+ Overtime) $53,389	Non-Productive $13,801	Standby	$5,342	Variability	$5,342
		Maintenance	$8,459	Training	$1,781
				General Meetings	$890
				Breaks	$890
				Other Downtime	$4,897
	Productive $26,712	Making Calls	$26,712		

Source: Adapted from Klammer 1996

8.4 LEVER 4 – RESOURCE UNIT COSTS

The first financial lever is the cost to acquire or to employ resources. For equipment or facilities, depreciation (and possibly cost of capital) may represent the cost. For people, cost is represented by salaries, payroll taxes, and benefits.

Capacity is acquired in discrete units, as was discussed in Chapter 7. A piece of equipment must be purchased even if only 10% will be utilized. Similarly, an entire employee must be hired even when only 20% of one is needed.[45] Often, tradeoffs are required between demand requirements and capacity constraints due to the cost of obtaining or maintaining capacity.

Rather than simply looking at high cost resources, the Closed-Loop Model enables a unit cost analysis in context of the activity, resource capacity, and demand for the ultimate product or service. Some resources may have a high unit cost while their impact is minimal in the context of the whole organization. Conversely, some resources may have a low unit cost while their overall impact is significant. For example, the Closed-Loop Model will help to assess whether a small group of very expensive technicians used by one high margin product line may be a more economic investment than a large group of inexpensive technicians used by several low margin product lines.

---

[45] This discussion excludes the choice of hiring part-time employees or on-demand labor, and if equipment was included in this example, it would exclude the option of pay-per-use equipment. In actual situations, management should investigate the viability of these options.

Figure 8.10 continues extending the call center application, assuming that all of the changes from the first three levers are still in place.

The fourth lever changes the resource cost. Figure 8.10 shows that to retain quality employees, the organization had to increase salary levels to $52,000 per FTE, or $2,000 more than planned. The total resource cost increased by $360,000, which meant that profits dropped to $1,240,000.

Organizations can use the resource cost lever to examine important questions such as:

- What was the cost of overtime versus the cost of additional personnel?

- Do certain products or processes need to be redesigned to minimize use of expensive resources?

- What was the impact of changes in resource costs on overall profitability?

- Would a long-term contract reduce the cost of the resource?

If the Capacity Model was used to analyze capacity in lever three, then it can also provide cost information about capacity utilization in this situation. Table 8.9 identified the cost of non-productive capacity and could serve as the basis for a ranking mechanism of areas for improvement.

Figure 8.10: Incremental Impact of Actual Resource Cost

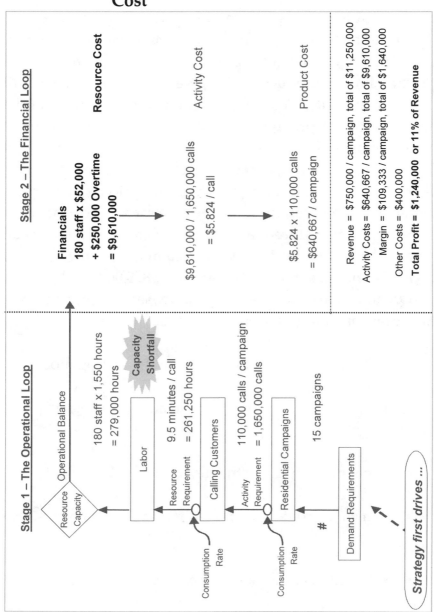

8.5 LEVER 5 – PRODUCT/SERVICE PRICING

The last lever is the pricing of products and services. In the planning process, assumptions were made concerning discounts and customer price sensitivity, perhaps at a product line or product family level. At whatever level of granularity those assumptions were made, the impact of the actual prices of products and services versus the planned prices can be significant.

Figure 8.11 completes the extended example by reflecting changes in the last lever: product/service prices. To increase demand to 15 campaigns, the average price of each campaign was reduced from $750,000 to $725,000. Total revenues dropped by $375,000 (15 campaigns times $25,000 each) showing that the final profit was $865,000.

Organizations can use the product/service pricing lever to address significant questions such as:

- What are the key components of the pricing model?

- Is product line pricing adequate to meet profit targets?

- What products have the most pricing flexibility?

- Which customer relationships have the most stable pricing?

- Are customer discounts appropriate?

Figure 8.11: Incremental Impact of Actual Service Prices

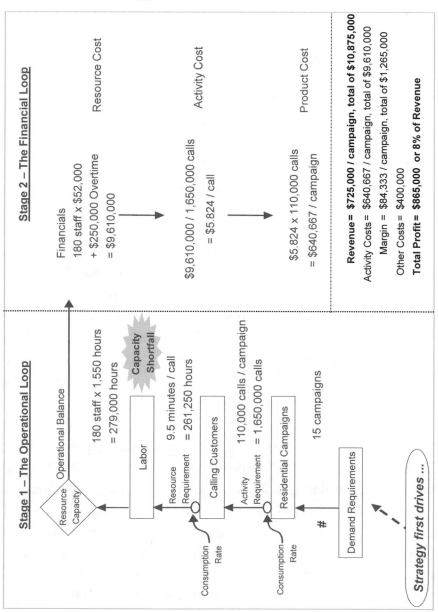

- Which products should be re-priced?

- What changes should be made in how customers are served in order to reduce cost and improve profitability?

- How did the change in pricing change the profitability of products and customers?

- What is the price elasticity of demand of each product? Is this elasticity the same upward as it is downward?

Traditional practices would analyze pricing as an independent variable. However, analysis based on the Closed-Loop Model shows how revenues and costs, activities, demands, and resources are inter-related. The Closed-Loop Model effectively prevents an organization from simply incorporating new product/service prices into a budget without forcing an examination of the resulting changes in the other levers.

The updated numbers from the Closed-Loop Model can be used to demonstrate the advantage of this approach. The actual results of the call center were that it lost $235,000 versus its initial plan as a result of all the changes throughout the period. If these changes in performance had all been known or even tested through scenario analysis, then the Closed-Loop Model could accurately have predicted this business result. In sharp contrast, a traditional margin analysis would have shown that the three additional marketing campaigns would each have a margin of $100,000, for a profit *improvement* of *$300,000*, and would not have been able to reflect the financial implications of most of the other changes that occurred. [46]

A comparison of all five levers is a key management input, and is shown in Table 8.12. Further analysis of the difference between the planned and actual results provokes additional questions concerning who has the responsibility for each lever and the results. Usually these questions can be more easily answered after examining management responsibilities and viewpoints.

8.6 MANAGEMENT RESPONSIBILITIES AND VIEWPOINTS

Analyzing the differences between actual and planned results has two distinct purposes. The first is as an aid to decision-making where the information can help the organization identify areas that need improvement. Quick analysis allows fast, real-time, adjustments. The second use is as a performance evaluation and measurement system where the information is used to reward managers and teams (as discussed in detail in Chapter 13).

Tying together the decision-making and performance systems has benefits and costs. When they are tied together, they align managers' incentives. Conversely, linking the two

---

[46] This gross margin is calculated as the base year margin of $125,000/campaign less the $25,000 price reduction for next year, for each of the three incremental campaigns. Management would of course have recognized that the price reduction applies equally to the initial 12 campaigns.

Table 8.12: Impact of Progressively Adding in Actual Performance for Each Lever

	# (A)	Campaigns Revenue — Per Campaign $000's (B)	Campaigns Revenue — Total $000's (C = A×B)	Calls — Per Campaign $000's (D)	Calls — Total $000's (E = A×D)	Min/Call (F)	Calls — Total $000's (G = E×F)	Total Hours $000's (H = G/60)	Total Staff (I)	Hrs/Staff (J)	Available Hours $000's (K = I×J)	Buffer — Hrs $000's (L = K−H)	Buffer — Staff FTE (M = L/J)	Salary/Staff $000's (N)	Resource Costs $000's (O)	Activity $/Call (P = O/E)	Per Campaign — Cost $000's (Q = D×P)	Per Campaign — Activity Profit $000's (R = B−Q)	Other Costs $000's (S)	Total Profit $000's (T = C−O−S)	% of Rev (U = T/C)
Base Scenario	12	$750	$9,000	100	1,200	10	12,000	200	150	1,500	225	25.00	16.7	$50	$7,500	6.25	$625.0	$125	$400	$1,100	12.2%
Lever 1 – Demand Quantities																					
Increase Campaigns / Add Staff to maintain balance	3		$2,250		300		3,000	50	30		45	-5.00	-3.3		$1,500						
Summary	15	$750	$11,250	100	1,500	10	15,000	250	180	1,500	270	20.00	13.3	$50	$9,000	6.00	$600.0	$150	$400	$1,850	16.4%
Lever 2 – Consumption Rates																					
10% Activity consumption increase / 5% drop in Resource consumption rate				10	150	-1	-825	-14	10		15	3.75	2.5								
Summary	15	$750	$11,250	110	1,650	10	15,675	261	190	1,500	285	23.75	15.8	$50	$9,500	5.76	$633.3	$117	$400	$1,350	12.0%
Lever 3 – Resource Capacity																					
Work overtime to use less people									-10	50	-15 / 9	-15.00 / 9.00	-10.0 / -4.4		-$500 / $250						
Summary	15	$750	$11,250	110	1,650	10	15,675	261	180	1,550	279	17.75	11.5	$50	$9,250	5.61	$616.7	$133	$400	$1,600	14.2%
Lever 4 – Resource Unit Cost																					
Salary Increase														$2	$360						
Summary	15	$750	$11,250	110	1,650	10	15,675	261	180	1,550	279	17.75	11.5	$52	$9,610	5.82	$640.7	$109	$400	$1,240	11.0%
Lever 5 – Product / Service Pricing																					
Reduce Price of Each Campaign		-$25																-$25			
Final	15	$725	$10,875	110	1,650	10	15,675	261	180	1,550	279	17.75	11.5	$52	$9,610	5.82	$640.7	$84	$400	$865	8.0%

can also lead to gaming. The appropriate level of integration varies from organization to organization. While there is no perfect solution, *understanding* the risk can help *reduce* the risk.

Identifying who or which function within each organization is responsible for managing each of the levers is critical. For example, sales and marketing managers may own the demand forecast and product/service pricing levers. In this case, they are responsible for both forecasting demand and delivering the forecasted volumes. Because demand volume is the first lever, the effects of deviations from the plan can be both significant and pervasive.

On the other hand, operating managers have little impact on the demand forecast but have responsibility for the processes and capacity to deliver the right product at the right time and at the right quality. Yet the ultimate cost of products/services can be dramatically affected by deviations from the demand forecast. Often, operating managers must commit to capacity decisions significantly in advance of actual delivery of that capacity and even more in advance of its use. When the forecasted demand does not materialize, who is responsible for the unused capacity and its cost? In many cases, such as those where long lead times for capacity acquisition are the norm, the responsibility for those costs perhaps should be primarily that of sales and marketing managers, not the operating managers.

Once demand quantity and price are established, operating managers have primary responsibility for the remaining levers: consumption rates, capacity, and resource costs. While there is a possibility that some sales and marketing decisions will affect operating processes, operating management has the task of operating processes efficiently, optimizing capacity, and obtaining resources at economical cost. Even when sales and marketing decisions impact operations, operating managers should use the Closed-Loop Model to first understand the impact of those decisions, and then communicate that impact to sales and marketing. Finally, the groups should jointly make appropriate decisions concerning the financial levers, commensurate with the organization's strategy.

While examining deviations from the internal budget benchmark or baseline is useful, it is only part of the picture. Management has many other sources of information it can and should use to manage the organization, its personnel, and expenses. The Closed-Loop Model is still just one tool - albeit an important tool - out of many.

At this stage in the implementation of the ABPB Process, an organization will have developed an initial Closed-Loop Model and assessed it against actual results. The next step is to apply the knowledge gained in developing and managing the Closed-Loop Model to turn it into the self-sustaining ABPB Process, the subject of Chapter 9 in this book.

9

CHAPTER

The ABPB Process: Sustaining the Closed-Loop Model

Having the building blocks in place and developing the initial Closed-Loop Model are important first steps towards success. The next steps are to add in the supporting elements that turn the calculation engine, the Closed-Loop Model, into a self-sustaining business process, the ABPB Process, that is understood and accepted by the entire organization. For the purposes of this book, "a sustainable process" is one that is:

- Used systemically,

- Continually improved and refined,

- Understood throughout the organization via training and documentation,

- Accepted throughout the organization as credible and valuable,

- Managed and developed by the process owner, and

- Desired by senior leadership.

Achieving a sustained ABPB Process is not a simple task. The organization must implement the key elements that support the Closed-Loop Model while managing the change as the organization switches to this new approach to planning and budgeting.

This chapter splits this task into two parts. It first defines the elements required to sustain the Closed-Loop Model, and then discusses how to manage the organizational changes needed to realize that goal.

9.1 THE SUPPORTING ELEMENTS OF THE ABPB PROCESS

The ABPB Process is shown in Figure 9.1. Like a waterfall, the ABPB Process is a cycle involving updating the basic structure of the Closed-Loop Model, calculating the current scenario, using the output from the calculations, and then collecting information to again revise the basic structure. The ABPB Process runs continuously, across all periods, with supporting elements both providing information to and drawing information from each iteration of the Closed-Loop Model.

The Closed-Loop Model is the calculation engine that lies at the heart of the process, and is designed to represent a specific time period, say a fiscal quarter or year. The Closed-Loop Model requires six supporting elements in order to

Figure 9.1: The CAM-I ABPB Process

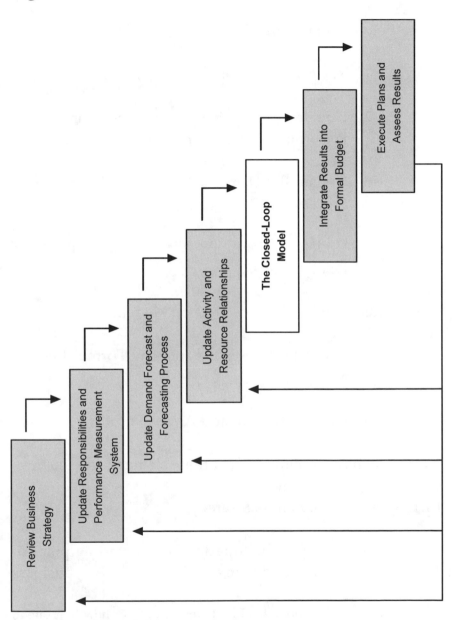

become the self-sustaining ABPB Process:

- Before Running the Closed-Loop Model:

    1. Review the Business Strategy,

    2. Update the Responsibilities and the Performance Measurement System,

    3. Update the Demand Forecast and Forecasting Process, and

    4. Update the Activity and Resource Relationships.

- After Running the Closed-Loop Model:

    5. Integrate the Results into the Formal Budget, and

    6. Execute the Plan and Assess Results.

We will now examine each of these elements in sequence.

9.1.1 Review the Business Strategy

Business strategy is the foundation and starting point of the planning and budgeting process.[47]   As business

---

[47] While this book does not intend to define strategy or how to create it, the four core elements of strategy are: defining the markets to serve,

conditions are continually changing, strategies need to be updated to recognize these changes. To review a business strategy means understanding the current state of business conditions and knowing the desired state of business outcomes. The review may be as simple as realizing that the prior strategy is still acceptable, or as complex as creating an entirely new business approach.

9.1.2 Update the Responsibilities and the Performance Measurement System

Organizations evolve over time. Both positions and individual responsibilities can shift over the course of a period. For example, business units can be combined, staff can be reorganized, production processes modified or discontinued, product lines added, and so on. In all of these situations, the individual responsibilities and the performance measurement system must change.

In order to reflect the operational and budgetary implications of such changes, particularly those affecting resources, the organization's performance measurement system (and perhaps the metrics themselves) must also change. The ABPB process is a core element in identifying these changes and it is important to maintain the integration across the key strategic management processes, as described further in Chapter 13.

---

identifying the products/services, deciding on processes and activities, and determining the relevant resources.

9.1.3 Update the Demand Forecast and Forecasting Process

Demand quantities are essential to the ABPB process, and therefore the demand forecasting process is also critical. There are two types of updating that may be required. The first is the essential step of updating the model period's demand forecast prior to actually running the Closed-Loop Model. This is required to drive the initial activity and resource requirements.

The second type is to examine the demand forecasting *process* itself to determine if it still meets the organization's requirements. An examination is particularly important if the prior period's demand forecasts varied substantially from actual demand levels. In this situation, care must be taken to differentiate process errors from data errors. Process errors reflect flaws in how the demand forecast is created and data passed on; data errors may mean that one or more assumptions was inappropriate, or that one or more data elements was incorrect, but that the process itself functioned appropriately. However appropriate the results, organizations should periodically assess their demand forecasting process. For instance, newer technologies such as data mining may enable more accurate or more in-depth forecast data than was previously the case.

9.1.4 Update the Activity and Resource Relationships

Product/service changes and process changes occur continuously in most organizations. For instance, new products/services are introduced, old production processes are modified or scrapped, new service delivery capabilities may be created, and new resources may become available. All of these changes may affect the relationships between activities, processes, resources, and the determination of capacity. Recognizing and capturing these changes is an important part of updating the Closed-Loop Model.

A second type of updating is determining the values of current parameters, such as increasing the cost of a specific resource from, say, $15 to $20 per unit.

9.1.5 Run the Closed-Loop Model

Once the Closed-Loop Model's underlying demand, activity, and resource relationships have been updated, and the latest values entered, the organization will run the Closed-Loop Model described in Chapters 2 and 3. The ultimate output will be the balanced operating and financial plans that the organization can use throughout the next period.

9.1.6 Integrate the Results into the Formal Budget

When a Formal Budget is required, the results from the Closed-Loop Model are transferred to the Formal Budget for review and approval, as described in Chapters 3 and 12.

9.1.7 Execute the Plans and Assess Results

Once the organization has accepted the plan, and potentially a Formal Budget, the organization will put the plan into practice. This is the natural starting and ending point of the planning cycle.

As the period progresses, actual performance will be measured and this information can be used to correct future actions (see Chapter 8), as well as to provide information that can be used to update and refine the Closed-Loop Model for the next cycle.

Comparing the actual to predicted results is one of the most powerful ways to update the Closed-Loop Model. Variances can be the result of many factors: inappropriate assumptions, incorrect assumptions about rates and measures, incorrect building blocks or links, or unpredictable events in the organization or the markets it serves. A careful and sequential analysis, as was shown in Chapter 8, can zero in on the appropriate reason for the variance, and, if appropriate, the Closed-Loop Model's parameters and linkages can be changed.

Because the ABPB Process deals in prediction and forecasting rather than certainty, and because there are so many factors that influence the demands for products and services and the rates at which activities and resources are consumed, no plan can ever *completely* match reality. The goal of the ABPB Process should *not* be to get the results *exactly* right, but rather to provide a model that the organization can rely on as a reasonably accurate predictor of future results. Therefore, the goal of the process manager or owner (see Section 9.2.1.1) should be to constantly improve the ABPB Process through each cycle and make the predicted results more closely approximate actual results.

The preceding paragraphs covered the core elements required to sustain the Closed-Loop Model. The ABPB Process is a new and improved approach to planning and budgeting that the organization will need to learn and use. As such, putting in place the physical infrastructure is not sufficient. Every implementation of the ABPB Process requires insightful change management.

9.2 CHANGE MANAGEMENT

Implementing the ABPB Process in any type of organization requires significant change management. Four major tasks are necessary to facilitate this change:

1. Transitioning from project management to managing the ABPB Process,

2. Developing a process that is not intrusive,

3. Managing applicable knowledge, and

4. Maintaining the visibility of the ABPB Process.

Most of these tasks should be incorporated into the Planning, Executing, and Closing stages of each project (see Chapter 6), but many will also continue once the ABPB Process is fully in place. These tasks should be undertaken in parallel and should be on-going through the life of the process. We will examine each in sequence.

9.2.1 Transitioning from Project Management to Managing the ABPB Process

The key success factors in transitioning from project to process management are:

- Forming the ABPB Process team,

- Documenting the ABPB Process, and

- Providing effective training.

9.2.1.1 Forming the ABPB Process Team

Once the ABPB Implementation Project is well underway, the project management team should begin to plan for the hand-off of the completed project to the person or team who will run the ABPB Process, which is termed the ABPB Process Team. There are many similarities between the selection of this team and the initial project team. Both teams should include representatives from multiple disciplines and functions across the organization. The team members should have the appropriate level of authority to make decisions and execute those decisions, and be able to bring obstacles and other issues to executive management. However, the key difference between the teams is that the ABPB Implementation Team was focused on completing a specific implementation, while the ABPB Process Team is focused on making sure that everything will be in place when they receive the hand-off from the ABPB Implementation Team.

It is a mistake to wait until the last minute to identify the team that will be running the new ABPB Process. Since the new process will be their on-going job, the ABPB Process Team members will be extremely interested in debugging the Closed-Loop Model and supporting elements. After all, they would be the ones that have to live with a poor design in the future!

The ABPB Process Team leader, or process manager/owner, will likely be a different person than the initial project or program leader since the skills and responsibilities for building a Closed-Loop Model are different than those of running one. The first key difference is that one role was that of a project manager, meaning a job responsibility with a specific set of objectives and time limits, while the process manager is an on-going role likely involving personnel management,[48] broader management briefings, technology maintenance and management, etc. But as with the project manager, the process team leader must have sufficient authority and respect to be able to work with all disciplines in the organization as well as sufficient flexibility to be able to deal with the inevitable teething pains of the new system.

---

[48] It is assumed here that the project manager does not have full personnel management responsibility for his or her team, but rather provides performance feedback and day-to-day direction during the course of the project. Once the project is complete, or in this situation, handed over to the process manager, both the project manager and the project team members return to their "home" functions or units.

9.2.1.2 Documenting the ABPB Process

Once the objectives of the ABPB Process have been agreed upon, the steps for the process must be documented. The ABPB Process documentation needs to be concise, easy to understand, and easily accessible to those who are involved in executing the process (the ABPB Process Team).[49] Process documentation is important because both team members and business users will frequently refer back to the documentation to understand how and why design decisions were made.

9.2.1.3 Providing Effective Training

Training in the ABPB Process is vital. There are two types of training. The first is educating the members of the ABPB Process team on their new duties. The ABPB Process and the role of participants should be clearly understood to ensure the success of the process. Thus, education regarding the ABPB Process should include information about the benefits of the process to the organization as a whole and to each individual, including information such as *why* the process is beneficial and how individual employees *fit* into the ABPB Process.

The second type of training is educating the members of the organization at large in the new process. All employees

---

[49] During the implementation of the ABPB Process, existing processes and documentation should be used wherever possible. The more the ABPB Process can build upon existing and proven processes, the easier it will be for those who are comfortable with the existing processes to become comfortable with and accept the ABPB Process.

have a vested interest in the financial success of an organization; consequently, most employees would like to know how the organization's plans match with their roles in those plans.

9.2.2 Developing a Process That Is Not Intrusive

Organizational changes often fail when they are too complicated, too labor intensive, or take individual contributors too far from their comfort zone. Therefore, a key recommendation towards the success of the ABPB Process is to develop a relatively simple one, expand on it over time, and seek to automate repetitive and error-prone tasks whenever it is cost-effective to do so. While planning and budgeting should be important to many employees in an organization, it's not their primary responsibility. Any process, especially a supporting one, must have minimal impact on employees' principal responsibilities.

Automation can be one of the keys to the success of the Closed-Loop Model. Automation and a well-defined process ease the burden on individual employees, and, when properly implemented, add a level of consistency and rigor to the Closed-Loop Model. Investing in the right set of tools to implement the ABPB Process and to automate appropriate portions of the process is certainly worthwhile (See Chapter 11). Most organizations already have systems in place that collect much of the data needed for a planning and budgeting model. Integrating the Closed-Loop Model with these systems can ease the burden on individuals and ensure that consistent, reliable data is being fed into the Closed-

Loop Model. Where legacy systems that perform needed functions are insufficient, new solutions may need to be identified, implemented, and integrated.

Thus, the key elements of a non-intrusive process are that the process itself seems to make sense to users as well as implementers, that the workload required to implement and maintain it is fairly conveyed to affected employees, that the pace of implementation not exceed what circumstances suggest, and that the implementation not seek to build in all the bells and whistles on day one when a basic model or process would suffice.

9.2.3 Managing Applicable Knowledge

Data is useless when it is disorganized or inaccessible. Data in a binder on a desk, while possibly useful to the owner of the desk, adds little to the organization's body of knowledge. *Knowledge management* is the process by which an organization effectively captures and *reuses* all of its knowledge thus *transforming* data into information, and information into knowledge that can be accessed, used, and understood throughout the organization.

To be effective, the ABPB Process needs the data in binders and in the heads of many employees. Knowledge Management principles and methods should be used to capture the significant elements of the ABPB Closed-Loop Models and the ABPB Process. These elements include the strategy, business assumptions, consumption rates, tolerances, sensitivities, capacities, skill substitutions, prices, and costs.

Employees will contribute their valuable information to the knowledge management system only if it requires a minimum amount of effort and they gain personal benefit from the system.   Making the knowledge management system as easy and collaborative as possible is critical to the success of any implementation effort.

9.2.4 Maintaining the Visibility of the ABPB Process

Visibility means many things at different points in the ABPB Process.   At the outset, it means obtaining and demonstrating the support of executive management, including those at the business unit being initially modeled. Thereafter, it also means that this support be demonstrably continued, through whatever means suit the culture and style of the organization.

Once implemented, visibility also means that the questions asked of the process team – and the decisions made as a result of data provided by the Closed-Loop Model – be shared with the unit and the organization as a whole. Simply knowing that the information gleaned from the Closed-Loop Model is being used – and is valued – provides an impetus to the ABPB Project and Process Teams, and also facilitates obtaining support from other units or functions.

Finally, success and failure need to be recognized and handled appropriately.   Both should be rewarded, albeit in different ways.   Success is straightforward: celebrate and communicate.   Failure requires that the team and organization should learn the causes and demonstrate model improvement to ensure that the failure is not repeated.   This learning must also be celebrated and communicated. Let's look at the elements of visibility in greater detail.

Understanding that the information in the ABPB Process is valuable and that the information is used to make business decisions is critical for senior management. Uses of the information should be visible and successes that occur as a result of using the information should be acknowledged and communicated throughout the organization. Without compromising competitively sensitive or otherwise secure data, the organization should share uses and benefits of the ABPB data as widely as possible.

For example, the security agency discussed in Chapter 4, Section 4.2, might share with its staff how it used the Closed-Loop Model to identify resource constraints and possible funding/fee concerns, and then re-aligned activities to better meet its financial circumstances. Similarly, the call center described in Chapter 3 should share its success in making operational improvements to meet the increased demand.

In addition to understanding and using the ABPB information, decision makers need to ask relevant questions and follow up in areas where required. When senior executives ask constructive questions, they exhibit an interest as well as a long-term commitment to the process. The value of asking these types of questions is often grossly under-estimated. The fastest way to generate participation in and enthusiasm for a new process is to have senior management demonstrate deep interest. Conversely of course, a perceived lack of interest and/or lack of use will almost certainly kill the process, not by stopping work effort but by destroying the morale of the team members and users of the Closed-Loop Model.

When implementing the ABPB Process, it is vitally important that successes be rewarded. It is even more important that mistakes be quickly and effectively addressed. First, however, since the ABPB Process is trying to measure the future, one must differentiate between a mistake and a change in business conditions or assumptions. In the early uses of the ABPB Process, these mistakes may be mostly the result of incorrect or missing data (e.g. cost drivers and consumption rates). In later uses, the cause of most mistakes may be inconsistent data collection, sloppy knowledge management practices, and errors in data entry. Results that are wrong should not be defended. Rather, effort should be applied to determining why the results were wrong and what needs to be done to correct the problem. The underlying cause of the error needs to be identified and proper action taken. All those affected by the error need to be made aware of the issues as well as the actions that are underway to prevent future occurrences. Problems that are addressed in a non-confrontational but effective manner improve confidence that the entire ABPB Process has value and is working properly.

Successfully sustaining an ABPB Process requires participation from all areas of the organization. Management must believe in the ABPB Process and must publicly approve and frequently endorse its implementation. Each employee must understand the importance that management places on the ABPB Process and participation from all contributors should be urged, if not mandated. In doing so, the organization might even consider rewarding the enthusiastic volunteer, not just the reluctantly compliant.

Through this chapter of the book, the reader has become familiar with the core requirements to sustain the ABPB Process. In order to complete this knowledge, Chapter 10 details several important elements of the Closed-Loop Model.

10 CHAPTER

A DEEPER EXAMINATION OF THE BUILDING BLOCKS

Chapter 7 described the major building blocks of the Closed-Loop Model and how they should be defined and applied in each ABPB Implementation Project. This chapter further explores the development and definition of the building blocks in the following four categories:

- Defining and forecasting demand,

- Measuring consumption rates,

- Understanding complex activity interactions, and

- Understanding the relationship between the Closed-Loop Model's financial results and cash flows.

10.1 DEFINING AND FORECASTING DEMAND

10.1.1 Determining the Volume of Demand

In the Closed-Loop Model, the demand forecast has two

specific uses:

- For operational planning and balance, and

- As the basis for developing a revenue forecast, which is needed for the financial balance stage.

The critical definition to understand is the phrase "volume of demand" and specifically the word "demand" itself.   In the context of the Closed-Loop Model, *demand* refers to each product or service that requires the incremental undertaking of at least one activity or the incremental consumption of the effort of at least one resource.[50] To illustrate how to define demand and to serve as a running example of additional concepts, a simplified adaptation of a real french-fry production facility is presented.[51]

---

[50] An alternate definition is that a demand is a product or service that cannot be made and/or delivered solely through the use of already performed activities solely using existing resources. Demands that can be met with existing inventory are not relevant to this discussion. In other words, the demand requires the incremental consumption of activities and/or resources.   Thus, a by-product of a production process is not a demand, at least for the purposes of estimating resource requirements in the production process.

[51] This example is simplified from one of the author's experience with a global producer of french fries and other food products. As with other examples in this book, the organization cannot be named for confidentiality reasons.

The French Fry Example – I

The production facility is required to produce only "Grade A" fries. The raw material needed to produce the fries, the potatoes, are of varying grades. Therefore, it is inevitable that some lower grade, yet still saleable, fries will be produced and that the production of these lower grade fries cannot be avoided. The expected quantity of lower grade fries that will be produced can be estimated using statistical techniques, based on the total quantity of potatoes entering the process. However, beyond what is needed to produce the Grade A fries, the production facility does not consume incremental activities or resources to produce lower grade fries. Therefore, *at least for production purposes*, lower-grade fries need not be included as demands in the Closed-Loop Model and the expected demand for lower grade fries is not an incremental demand quantity. In this example, the manufacturing process should be modeled using only the demand for Grade A fries as lower grade fries are a by-product of Grade A production.

In contrast to the manufacturing process, the packaging process will likely require that each grade of fries be uniquely identified and their volumes estimated separately. This is because the packaging of lower-grade fries will likely result in additional activities being performed and will certainly result in additional and likely different materials being ordered and used.

Using the appropriate consumption rates is of critical importance. Consider the impact of incorrectly considering lower grade fries as a demand. Assume that each 100 units of Grade A fries produced typically results in 10 units of lower grade fries being produced. If the consumption rate for the activity "make fries" is 1 per 10 units of *fries*, then the activity quantity will be 11 (calculated as 1 activity occurrence for every 10 units of fries, with a total of 110 units of fries being produced). But this is incorrect!

Only Grade A fries require production resources, and thus the correct activity consumption rate is 1 per 10 units of *Grade A fries*. A critical observation is that it is not just the *numerical rate* that is different but also the *metric itself* (per 10 units of *Grade A fries*, not per 10 units of *fries*).

The key conclusion from this example is that the definition of demand varies with the specific application or resource area at hand. It is not relevant whether the demand is handled by the same resource, but rather whether each resource must differentiate its work effort (activity or time) across more than one demand item. Figure 10.1 indicates the unique elements of demand.

Figure 10.1: Unique Elements of Demand

Does the product require incremental resources?

YES	Identify Uniquely	Identify Uniquely
NO	Do Not Identify Uniquely	Identify Uniquely
	NO	**YES**

Does this product require a new activity or incremental volume of an existing activity?

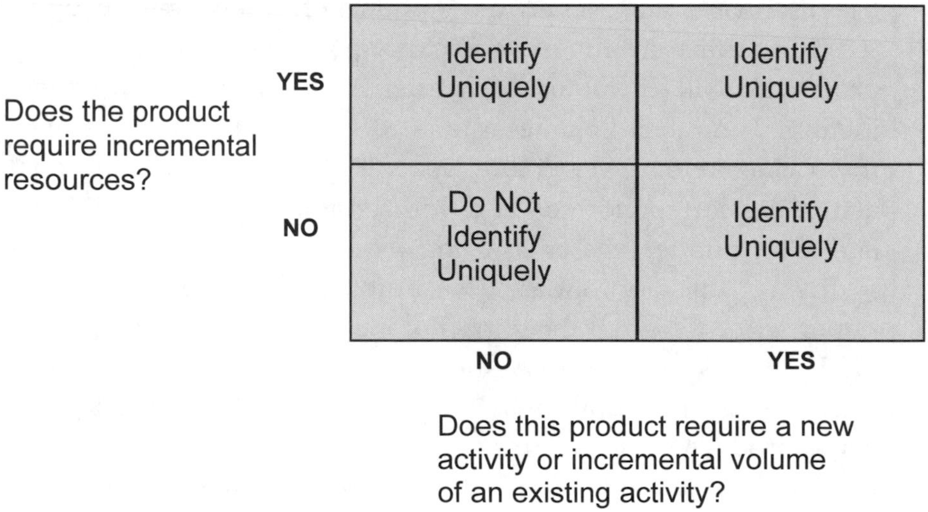

The definition of "volume" follows from that of demand. While this may appear to be straightforward, it too depends on the resource at issue. Again, the french-fry production facility example will be used to illustrate this point.

The French Fry Example – II

To determine the quantity of resources required for bulk manufacturing, the resource planner may find it sufficient to know the total monthly or annual production quantity (number of pounds of fries). However, other planners, such as those responsible for production scheduling, may also need to know the planned size or length of each production run. Going further, some planners will find it sufficient to know the planned monthly or annual volume for each grade, while other planners may require knowledge of demand by package size and printing format.

Thus, the level of detail required for demand quantity will change depending on the activity and resource under consideration. An organization may have deeper levels of detail for each element of demand, with each level of detail being used for a specific purpose.

Figure 10.2 depicts how demand volume should be defined at incremental levels of granularity, moving through an organization from highly aggregate plans to more micro-level plans.

The level of granularity at which demand volumes must be known increases with the level of detail at which an employee works. For example, staff responsible for aggregate production and/or equipment capacity may not be

Figure 10.2: Granularity of Demand Knowledge

	Equipment Capacity	Product Marketing	Production Scheduling	Materials Management
Total Demand				
By Grade				
By Period				
By Size				

concerned with demand by grade or package size, whereas those responsible for materials management likely do need that information.

Once the demand forecast is finalized, the organization can then complete the operational balance stage of the Closed-Loop Model, including any required changes to the demand forecasts. The balanced demand forecast is then used to derive the revenue forecasts.

10.1.2 Applying and Using Revenue Forecasts

The *revenue forecast* is the expression of a demand volume forecast in terms of the unit of currency of the organization. Therefore, the dollarized demand volume reflects the unique price and/or volume combination for each item of demand, and the revenue forecast represents the sum of each element of dollarized demand volume. At a minimum, it must be recognized that the same demand item may be sold to customers at different prices.

Revenue forecasts are easier to understand in situations where the provider and consumer are different entities, i.e. in cases where an invoice will be issued to a third-party for the demand, rather than in internal environments where the establishment of price is more complex. The example of the french-fry production facility can be used to illustrate the concept of revenue forecasts.

The French Fry Example – III

In forecasting the revenues from selling the fries, it is not sufficient to consider only the total tonnage of Grade A fries produced but also:

- Total tonnage, by package format, package size, etc. expressed in the unit of sale,

- The breakdown of each of these volumes by sales market (country, region, sales channel, etc.), and

- Similar information with regards to the incremental sales from lower grade fries.

The revenue forecast must be managed at both the aggregate and the individual product, if not customer, level. The aggregate revenue is required at the end of the financial stage of the Closed-Loop Model, at the point where the financial results of the process are compared to the organization's financial targets.   As was discussed in previous chapters of this book, two possibilities emerge: either the plan delivers the target return or the plan fails to deliver the required results.

If the plan fails to deliver the required target level of profitability, then the detailed revenue forecast is useful in adjusting the volume of demand and/or prices to achieve the desired profitability levels. Changing product demands and revenues are two of the five levers, described in Chapter 8, that the Closed-Loop Model can use to achieve financial balance.

If the plan delivers the required financial results, it may appear that the detailed revenue forecast serves no further purpose. However, the detailed revenue forecast is still of substantial value.   Achieving financial balance at an organization-wide level may be sufficient to allow the plan to be completed, but this does not mean that each organizational unit (or product, market, channel, etc.) is in financial balance. While operational balance, by definition, is achieved at an individual resource level, the same is not necessarily true of financial balance. The organization may achieve its target, but individual units may be in or out of financial balance.

The final, detailed, product-level revenue forecast has at least one other use beyond resource planning. The detailed product-level forecast can be combined with the activity cost analysis to measure the profitability of any cost object (products, services, channels, etc.) that may be of concern to the organization.

10.1.3 The Role of Volume and Revenue Forecasting Tools and Techniques

There are many different types of forecasting tools available to support the prediction of demand volumes and/or revenues. This sub-section provides a brief commentary on how such approaches might be applied in an ABPB environment.

The most predictable relationships are often seen only through aggregation prior to statistical modeling. In the context of this french-fry example, it is unlikely that volume forecasts can be accurately developed at very low levels of the demand hierarchy (e.g. one pound bags of curly seasoned fries), but much more likely that such forecasts can be accurate at more aggregate levels (e.g. total volume of curly fries). Experience suggests that aggregate forecasts may be allocated to lower levels of the demand hierarchy using historical trends supplemented by current knowledge of planned events (e.g. promotions).

The example of the french-fry production facility can be used to demonstrate the features of a successful revenue forecast.

The French Fry Example – IV

The demand information for this example is as follows:

- Total forecasted volume for curly seasoned fries is 1,200 units per quarter.

- This forecasted volume is initially divided among package sizes based on historical information:

  a. 600 units in 1-pound bags,
  b. 300 units in 2-pound bags,
  c. 150 units in ½-pound bags, and
  d. 150 units in 5-pound bags.

- In the third quarter, aggressive pricing promotions are planned for the 5-pound bag product, such that this volume is expected to increase to 200 units, with the commensurate loss of 20 units each of 2-pound and 1-pound bags respectively.

- The planned promotion will not impact sales until the last month of the quarter.

Based on this information, the organization can conclude that the base volume of demand will occur for the first two months of the quarter but will change in the third month to reflect the impact of the planned promotion.

The next step is to convert this demand information into a revenue forecast. Again, it is usually appropriate to forecast unit revenue at an *average* level, such as $5.00 per bag, rather than trying to divide the expected volume among all of the potential customers for that product.

Consider for a moment the complexities involved in trying to forecast at the customer level. In that situation, the monthly forecast would have to be split by customer and a unique price applied to each account. Not only is the effort required to generate the information far greater, but the absolute number of differences and the potential for error will almost certainly be greater. What are the odds of getting the volume *and* price correct for each customer, *and do so by month*, versus getting the aggregate volume and average price correct? For these reasons, forecasting at a more aggregate level is usually superior.

Macro-economic data is also significant in the development of most forecasts, both to predict demand volumes as well as sales revenues. However, such data is of primary benefit in predicting overall annual trends for industry growth, and less so for individual business results or seasonal volumes and/or revenues.

Next, there is the important issue of making sure that the users of forecasts are satisfied with the forecasts being developed for them. Several practices contribute to increasing user satisfaction:

- Increase the frequency of forecasts,

- Focus on the bottom line, meaning high margin items, low volume but big ticket items, high profile items, and items with complementary product relationships,

- Hold the forecasters and forecasting process accountable, in part by tracking performance and quantifying errors,

- Improve the forecast process systematically rather than as part of an annual event,

- Communicate changes and results in a timely manner,

- Improve data sources on a continual basis, which also requires prompt and direct feedback to providers of data,

- Communicate assumptions, and

- Issue only one coordinated forecast for the organization or at least reconcile multiple forecasts from different functions.

Finally, knowledge of the product lifecycle can greatly aid forecast allocation decisions. Knowing where products and competitors' products are in their lifecycle helps planners predict the impact of any new promotions, launches, etc.

10.1.4 Transfer Prices

Revenue forecasts are fairly easy to understand in situations where an invoice will be issued for the demand. The development of demand and revenue forecasts for business units whose customers are internal to the organization and where products and services are not priced at market rates is more complex.[52] This situation leads to what are called *transfer prices*.

In situations where the seller can largely dictate the transfer price,[53] the buyer's ability to pay the unit price might drive the initial estimate of, or commitment to, a volume level for the unit. For example, if the buyer has a total budget of $100, then a unit price of $5 will lead to an initial demand projection of 20 units. However, if the seller only has 10 units available, then there will be unfilled demand at the price of $5 per unit. In this case, the seller raises the price to $10 per unit, which generates a buyer's demand of 10 units and again costs $100 (the buyer's entire budget). The powerful seller sets a price to extract the entire budget from the buyer and meet operational balance.

Conversely, if the buyer can dictate the unit price and its volumes, then the seller must take its revenues as fixed. For example, the buyer purchases 40 units and pays $3 per unit. Faced with a volume of 40 units and total revenue of $120, the seller must achieve operational and financial balance solely using internal variables, such as its cost structure and process efficiencies.

The two polar situations discussed above do not occur very often in internal markets. In most circumstances, the

---

[52] If market rates are used for internal transactions, there is no issue of affordability. The internal provider's prices will be the same as any other provider and therefore the buyer must work with the price as a given.

[53] There are two natural settings where this can occur. The first is the case where the seller is a monopolist, while the second case is where corporate policy sets transfer prices based on the selling unit's financial requirements or targets.

buyer and seller seek mutually beneficial volumes and prices, with perhaps both parties looking externally to sell greater volumes or procure certain products or services. In internal markets, as in third-party situations, buyers and sellers may also negotiate a lengthy list of product/service elements beyond price and quality, such as service level, and volume commitments in developing agreements and budgets.

10.2 MEASURING CONSUMPTION RATES

The consumption rates used in the Closed-Loop Model assume that the organization has developed links between demands and activities, and between activities and resources. Linking demands, activities, and resources was introduced in Chapter 7. This section discusses how to deal with fixed and variable consumption rates.

10.2.1 Estimating Fixed Consumption Rates

A simple approach to estimating consumption rates can be used when the consumption rate is fixed or varies within a very narrow range: the organization can use a fixed value. An excellent example of this situation occurs in the airline industry.

The Airline Example – I

In commercial aviation, a regulator, such as the Federal Aviation Administration, specifies the interval between aircraft inspections. For example, each aircraft must undergo an examination of pre-determined rigor after a specified number of takeoffs or flying hours. For the purposes of this example, an examination must take place after every 1,000 flight hours. Thus, the consumption rate for this example can be developed as follows:

- If demand is expressed in flight hours, then every flight hour consumes 1/1,000th of the specified examination (i.e. the activity of "perform 1,000 hour maintenance examination"). In this way, the organization can build up the quantity of resources required to support each flight hour; and

- If the organization using the Closed-Loop Model is an internal service provider, such as the maintenance function of the airline, then the demand may be the examination itself. In this case, this volume must be derived from or supplied by an external source. For example, the operations group might inform maintenance that 800,000 flight hours are planned. Using the activity consumption rate of 1 examination per 1,000 flight hours, the maintenance function can calculate that there will be 800 examinations. In turn, the maintenance function can develop consumption rates for each activity and/or task that comprises the examination, and thus can estimate the quantity of resources sufficient for the volume of activity.

While an airline might be permitted a narrow range of flight hours within which the examination must be performed, such as 970 – 1,030, the range is very narrow and the target value is mandated. In such cases, the most appropriate course of action is to treat the consumption rate as a fixed amount.

10.2.2 Managing Variability in Consumption Rates

Extreme variability in consumption rates can invalidate the Closed-Loop Model. If a consumption rate varies to the extent that it cannot be used to effectively plan activity or resource volumes, then that rate should not be used. If this particular rate is critical in arriving at a valid plan, then another approach should be used to generate the plan.

While extreme model-breaking variability may occur, it is more likely that the consumption rates will vary to some extent over the course of a period. The degree to which a rate varies may well determine the time period that the Closed-Loop Model can serve. There are two likely cases:[54]

- If rates vary widely month-to-month but are expected to be stable on an annual basis, then the Closed-Loop Model can be used to plan activity and resource volumes on an annual basis, but may not be effective in planning shorter term decisions.

---

[54] There is a potential difference between a peak and non-peak consumption rate and a peak and non-peak demand. These are advanced capacity issues not addressed in this book.

- If the Closed-Loop Model is run once a month, then using monthly rates that match the model's horizon are more valuable than average annual ones.

10.3 UNDERSTANDING COMPLEX ACTIVITY INTERACTIONS

In all budget systems, higher level (consumer) organizational units budget using aggregates of the lower level (supplier) units' demands, activities, and resources.[55] For example, flight operations, the consumer unit in the airline example, might budget resources using a measure such as "examine aircraft". However, the maintenance department, the supplier, might take that measure and break it down into components of "check wheels", "check engines", etc. Aggregation is necessary to avoid overwhelming detail at upper levels, but it can lead to problems when using traditional budget systems. Traditional budgeting usually does not allow consumer units to update the demand volumes for supplier units in a quick and manageable fashion. Furthermore, in most traditional budgeting environments, various budgets of organizational units do not "talk" to each other. Each unit's budget is a silo unto itself, with thick walls separating its

---

[55] In this context, the terms "higher level" and "lower level" relate to a hierarchical perspective; that is, a parent company is a higher-level unit while a subsidiary or division is a lower-level unit. The terms "consumer" and "supplier" refer to typical purchaser and provider situations, whereby one unit provides demand information to another that in turn provides services and/or goods to meet that demand. Whether the relationship is internal or external is not relevant.

completion and results from that of other functions, and only the thinnest of absolutely essential linkages to other units' budgets. The results of lower level units' detailed activity and resource models are not available to upper levels of the organization. Similarly, the results of supplier units' models are not often visible to consumer units. Thus, when the organization-wide budget needs to be updated quickly, the upper level organization cannot access the detailed lower level models. Thus, most traditional budget processes are not "linked" or "networked." This situation is depicted in Figure 10.3.

Figure 10.3: Traditional Budget Walls

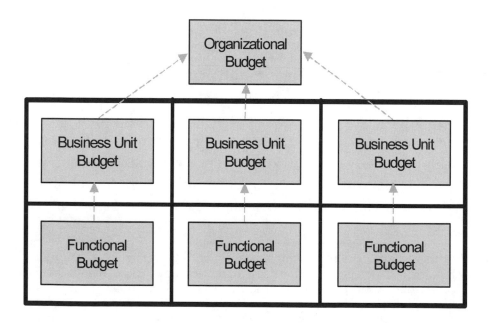

Conversely, a linked or networked budgeting process is one that feeds the results of supplier unit models into the appropriate points in the models of consumer units. This situation can occur in multiple situations, such as:

- One organizational unit provides support services to another, where both the provider and the consumer are at the same level in the organizational hierarchy. An example is the accounting department processing payroll for the manufacturing department;

- One organization unit sells goods to another, where the supplier is "lower" in the organizational hierarchy than the consumer. An example is a plant that manufactures a part sold to a division that assembles the parts into a finished product; and

- Independent organizational units roll up their budgets to a parent entity, which may only have aggregate budget authority over each subsidiary unit. An example is a government agency that provides a budget and spending authority to regional offices, but does not control how those funds are spent.

In all three of these cases, some aggregate reporting of results to the higher level or consuming organization is required. In the case of a service provider, it may be the unit cost and/or total cost along with total resource requirement; for a parts plant, it may only be unit cost; and for independent government agencies, it may be the total resource requirement and total financial requirement.

In contrast to traditional systems, the Closed-Loop Model resolves both of the limitations described earlier. Demands are automatically cascaded from the consumer unit's model down to the supplier unit's model.

Once the supplier unit obtains results, they are rolled up to the consumer unit. In more complex settings, lower level results roll up to intermediate unit Closed-Loop Models and, in turn, to the organization-wide Closed-Loop Model. Thus, the Closed-Loop Model can be viewed as a series of linked and networked models.

The concepts of cascading demands and networked Closed-Loop Models are shown in Figures 10.4 and 10.5 respectively.

The airline example is further developed to illustrate the concepts of cascading and linking, initially to show the limitations of traditional approaches and then to show the benefits of the Closed-Loop Model.

Figure 10.4: Cascading Demands From Consumer to Supplier Closed-Loop Models

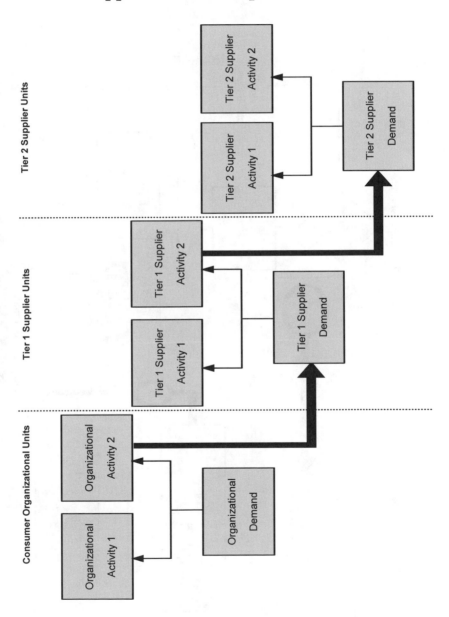

Figure 10.5: Feedback Through Networked Closed-Loop Models

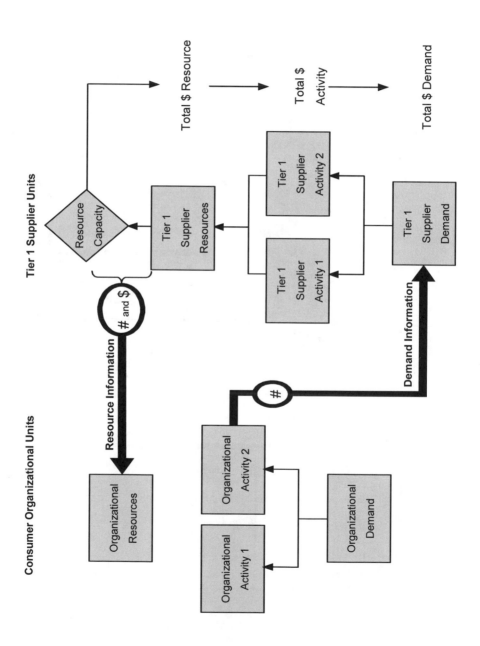

The Airline Example – II

The initial forecasts and assumptions at the upper level of the organization were as follows:

- Throughout most of the budget process, demand was estimated at 800,000 flight hours;

- The consumption rate is fixed by the regulator at 1 examination per 1,000 flight hours;

- Thus, the maintenance function can plan for, at a macro level, 800 examinations;

- Each examination requires an average of 2,500 direct labor hours, such that the maintenance function can estimate a total labor requirement of 2,000,000 hours;

- Based on a typical estimate of 1,500 labor hours per FTE per year plus 20 percent overtime allowance (i.e. 300 hours per FTE per year), the function can then plan for a resource requirement of 1,111 FTE (i.e. 2,000,000 hours divided by 1,800 hours per FTE), to which it then adds a nominal amount of buffer capacity for a total of 1,150 FTE; and

- The requirement of 1,150 FTE matched the current staffing level.

Figure 10.6 depicts the calculation of the initial resource requirements by the upper level of the organization, based on an average resource requirement for each "perform examinations" activity. The example also assumes that this model is in

Figure 10.6: Airline Example II: Calculating Upper Level Resource Requirements for Aircraft Maintenance

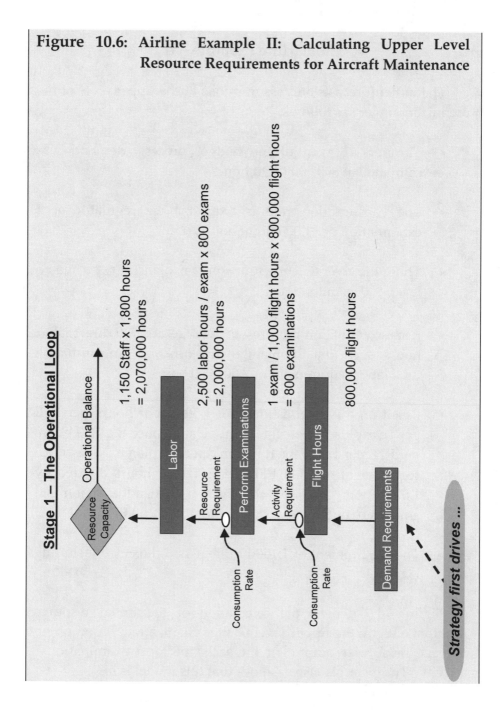

operational balance

The financial position of the organization is shown in Figure 10.7. The example is simplified by assuming that all of the costs of the maintenance function are fully charged to another function within the airline. Therefore, the maintenance function achieves financial balance immediately upon adding its costs to an operationally balanced model. It does not need to formally seek financial balance.

The expected resource, activity, and service costs are:

- Total labor cost is $82,800,000,[56] assuming that there are no other costs,

- Activity cost (per examination) is $103,500, and

- Service cost (per flight hour) is $103.50.

In this example, the service cost is expressed in the metric of the unit of demand, meaning that each flight hour "consumes" about $103.50 of maintenance examination costs.

Suppose that, very late in the budgeting process, the demand forecast is suddenly increased to 1,100,000 flight hours. The following paragraphs describe how an organization with traditional budget processes likely would handle this change. This is followed by an illustration of how linked Closed-Loop Models can improve upon the traditional budgeting process' relatively crude solution (see Section 10.3.1).

---

[56] Calculated as: 1,150 FTE at 1,500 worked hours plus 300 vacation, statutory holiday, and other paid absence hours, each at $30/hour equals $62,100,000; add 300 overtime hours per FTE at $60/hour equals $20,700,000; total equals $82,800,000.

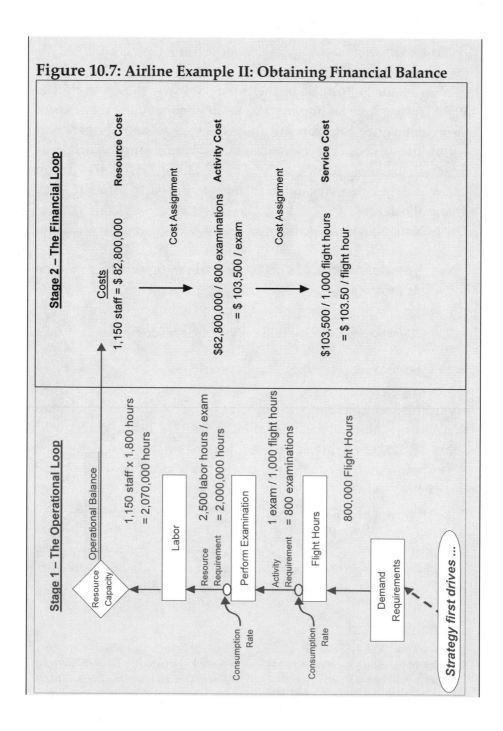

Figure 10.7: Airline Example II: Obtaining Financial Balance

In an organization with traditional budget processes, only a financial estimate of the impact of the increased demand at the aggregate level of the maintenance function would be considered. Extrapolating the maintenance cost per flight hour against the new demand level would be a common approach. Thus, most organizations would simply adjust their maintenance budget at this aggregate level as follows:

- Previous service cost times new volume level equals new budget, or

- $103.50 * 1,100,000 flight hours = $113,850,000.

Not surprisingly, this calculation represents a linear increase in the budget, perfectly proportional to the increase in demand volume. In contrast to the full flow of the Closed-Loop Model, most organizations act as if they "short-circuit" the operational side and immediately jump to a new financial budget (shown in Figure 10.8).[57]

---

[57] Most organizations do not plan or budget using this approach and would simply perform the mathematical calculations, not even recognizing that they have bypassed the Operational Loop.

Figure   10.8:   Airline   Example   II: Short-Circuiting   the   Operational Loop

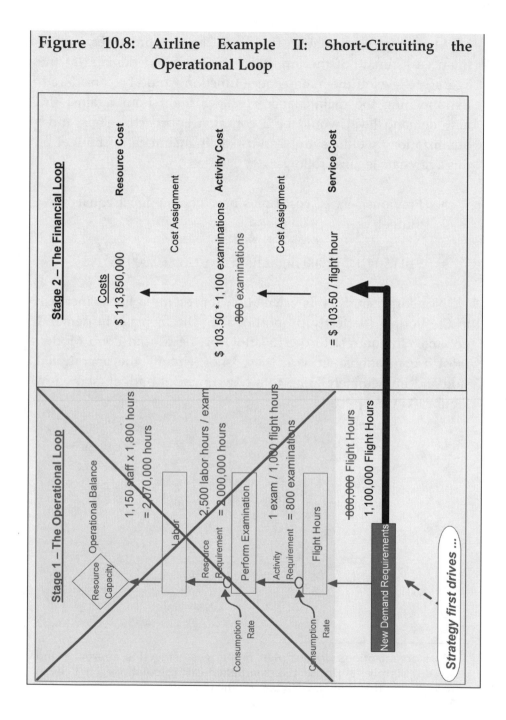

Many organizations take this simplified approach because demands cannot cascade from one unit to the next, and the organization's lower level budgeting models are not linked to the upper level ones. Thus results do not readily flow between levels of the organization.

10.3.1 Successfully Cascading Demands and Activities

The ABPB Process' cascading demands and networked Closed Loop Models allow the maintenance function to quickly estimate the operational and financial implications of the new demand volume.

There are six steps in updating a budget across linked Closed-Loop Models within an organization:

Step 1. The higher-level activities, as derived from higher-level demands and activity consumption rates, are passed down (cascaded to) the lower level units and become demands for these units.

Step 2. The lower-level demands are broken down into more discrete demands, ones for which the unit actually undertakes activities.[58]

---

[58] Note that Steps 1 and 2 (cascading demands and breaking them into appropriate unit level activities) may be repeated multiple times at ever-lower levels of the organization, until the process arrives at the level of the organization where end-item demands and/or services are delivered.

Step 3. The discrete demands are used to launch unit-level Closed-Loop Models, thus generating unit-level activity requirements.

Step 4. Through the algorithm of the Closed-Loop Model described earlier in this book, the unit activity requirements are translated into unit-level resource requirements and, once in operational balance, appropriate financial budgets are created.

Step 5. The individual resource requirements within a unit, or by demand, are aggregated for the unit as whole, and passed back to the upper level model (along with whatever other operational data is required).

Step 6. The costs for each resource within each lower level unit are aggregated to arrive at total unit resource costs, and these aggregate resource costs are passed back to the upper level model (along with whatever other financial data is required).

The following paragraphs and figures demonstrate these six steps in detail for the assumptions in Airline Example II, with 800 examinations, and then describe how an efficient update can be completed.

The Airline Example – III

Step 1

The cascading of demands is shown in Figure 10.9. In this case, the activity at the consuming unit, "Perform Examinations", becomes the demand at the supplier unit.

Step 2

The aggregate demand is broken down into more granular demands to identify those things for which the unit actually performs work; this dis-aggregation is quite similar to what takes place in strong ABCM implementations. In this example, the maintenance unit does not simply "Perform Examinations". Rather, it performs examinations on two different aircraft types: 2-engine and 4-engine aircraft. Since the labor requirements differ by aircraft type, the unit must break down the aggregate demand along these lines. This breakdown by aircraft type is shown in Figure 10.10.

This example assumes that the initial demand volume of 800,000 flight hours was met by:

- 550,000 flight hours on 2-engine aircraft (each with 8 tires),

- 250,000 flight hours on 4-engine aircraft (each with 12 tires), and

The examinations must be performed after each 1,000 flight hours for each type of aircraft.

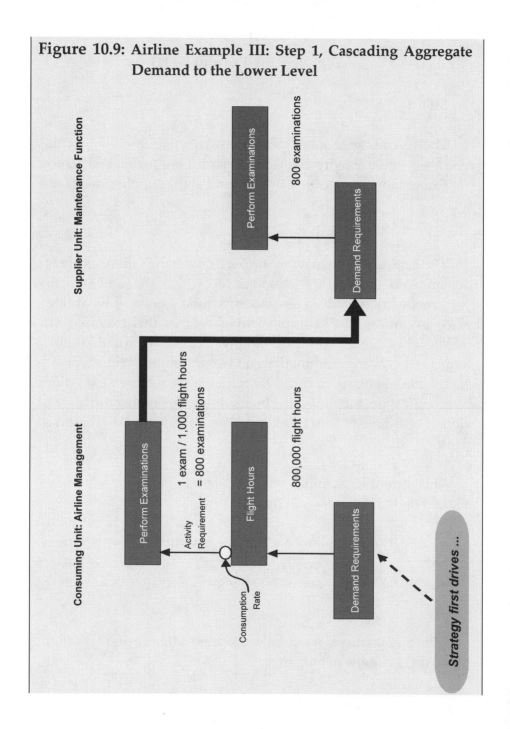

Figure 10.9: Airline Example III: Step 1, Cascading Aggregate Demand to the Lower Level

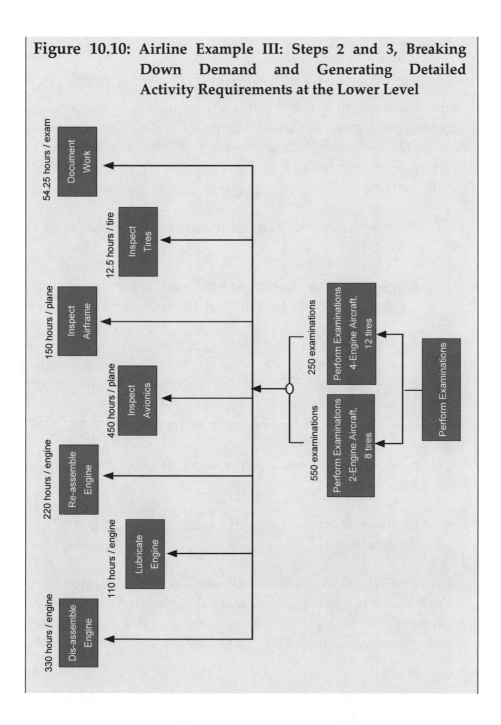

Figure 10.10: Airline Example III: Steps 2 and 3, Breaking Down Demand and Generating Detailed Activity Requirements at the Lower Level

Step 3

The next step is to identify the more detailed activities, which in total add up to a full 1,000-hour maintenance examination requiring an average of 2,500 labor hours. The seven activities needed for this example are listed below (the *italicized* words below provide the linkage to Figure 10.10). The maintenance function will:

1. *Dis-assemble engine* and components, at 330 hours per engine,

2. *Lubricate* and/or inspect *engine* and components and replace minor parts as needed, at 110 hours per engine,

3. *Re-assemble* and install *engine*, at 220 hours per engine,

4. *Inspect*, test, and adjust *avionics*, at 450 hours per aircraft,

5. *Inspect airframe*, at 150 hours per aircraft,

6. *Inspect tires* and replace as necessary, at 12.5 hours per tire, and

7. *Document work* and file with regulator, at 54.25 hours per examination.

This additional information allows the groups within the maintenance function to generate a detailed plan that captures the required mix of labor. The activity list shows that some of the consumption rates are "per engine," others are "per aircraft," another is "per tire," and a final one is "per examination".[59] This information was also shown in Figure 10.10. In traditional budgeting processes, a detailed breakdown rarely takes place, and almost certainly would not be adjusted in the circumstance of a change in the underlying level of demand.

Step 4

Figures 10.11 and 10.12 show the fourth step in the completion of these models: the generation of detailed lower level resource requirements for the 2-engine and 4-engine aircraft inspections respectively. The calculations are simple, although lengthy; in the case of the 2-engine aircraft (Figure 10.11), the total resource requirement is arrived at by summing up the following components:

- 330 hours/engine x 2 engines/plane x 550 examinations = 363,000 hours, plus

- 110 hours/engine x 2 engines/plane x 550 examinations = 121,000 hours, plus

- 220 hours/engine x 2 engines/plane x 550 examinations = 242,000 hours, plus

- 450 hours/plane x 550 examinations = 247,500 hours, plus

- 150 hours/plane x 550 examinations = 82,500 hours, plus

---

[59] In this example, "per aircraft" and "per examination" have the same consumption rate, because the aircraft itself is the object of the examination. If the documentation and regulatory filings, however, were by activity, this would not be the case.

Figure 10.11: Airline Example III: Step 4, Determining Resource Requirement, 2-Engine Aircraft Inspections

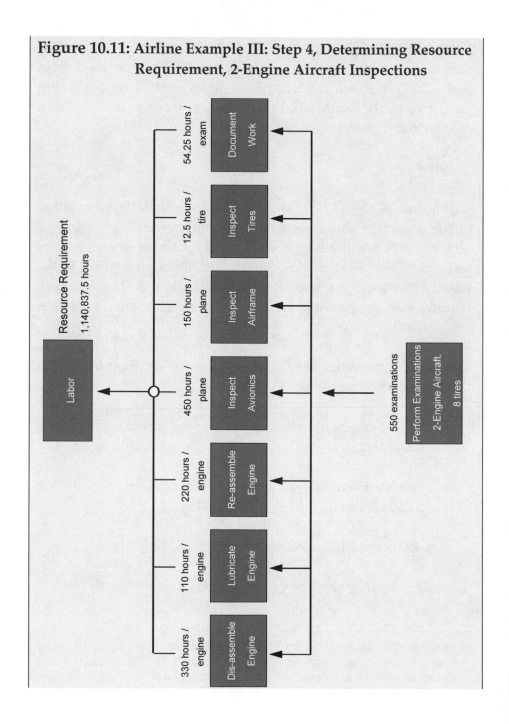

Figure 10.12: Airline Example III: Step 4, Determining Resource Requirement, 4-Engine Aircraft Inspections

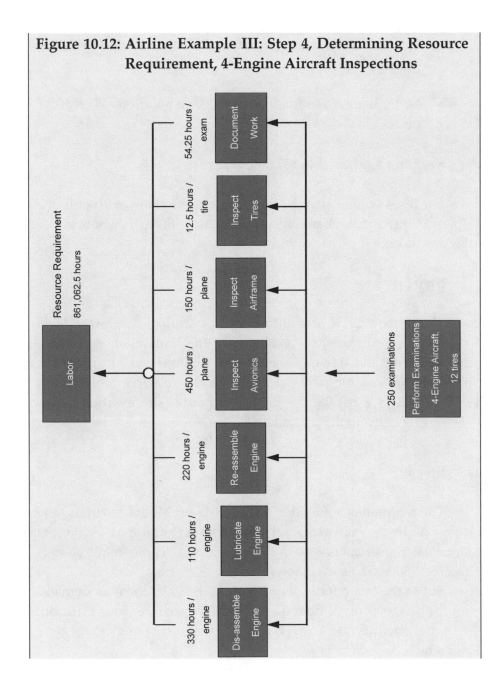

- 12.5 hours/tire x 8 tires/plane x 550 examinations = 55,000 hours, plus

- 54.25 hours/examination x 550 examinations = 29,837.5 hours,

- For a total of 1,140,837.5 hours.

For the 4-engine aircraft, the steps are the same, with only the specific quantities changing, and totaling 861,062.5 hours (see Figure 10.12).

Step 5

The fifth step is straightforward. Adding the lower level resource requirements results in the aggregate resource requirement, and this is passed to the higher level. In this case, the maintenance model would pass on the resource requirement of 1,140,837.5 + 861,062.5 = 2,001,900 hours (simply rounded to 2,000,000 hours) to the upper level.

Step 6

The maintenance function's Closed-Loop Model calculates the costs of these resources, aggregates them, and passes on the financial requirements to the upper level. These requirements total $82,800,000, as was shown earlier.

But at the last minute, as is so often the case, the new demand level (1,100,000 flight hours) is sent to the maintenance function, with the obvious question: How much will it cost to meet the new demand?

One possibility is that the maintenance department would re-run its model with the new parameters. However, in this example, there is a simpler method. All maintenance needs to know is the following revised piece of data:

- 600,000 flight hours will take place on 2-engine aircraft, and

- 500,000 flight hours will take place on 4-engine aircraft.[60]

Using this information, the lower-level maintenance function can generate the detailed activity and resource breakdowns shown in Figures 10.13 and 10.14.

The total resource requirement is now 1,244,550 + 1,722,125 = 2,966,675 hours. Using the same assumptions for workload, hourly rates, and overtime as was previously the case, the updated resource cost can be calculated as follows:

- 2,966,675 hours divided by 1,800 worked hours per FTE equals 1,648.2 FTE,

- Round up the FTE requirement by about the same ratio as previously, to 1,700 FTE,

- Each FTE is paid for 300 hours vacation etc., works 300 overtime hours, and

- Total resource cost is thus $122,400,000.

---

[60] This example is simplified to exclude the question of capacity, i.e. does the airline have the requisite number of planes, crews, etc.

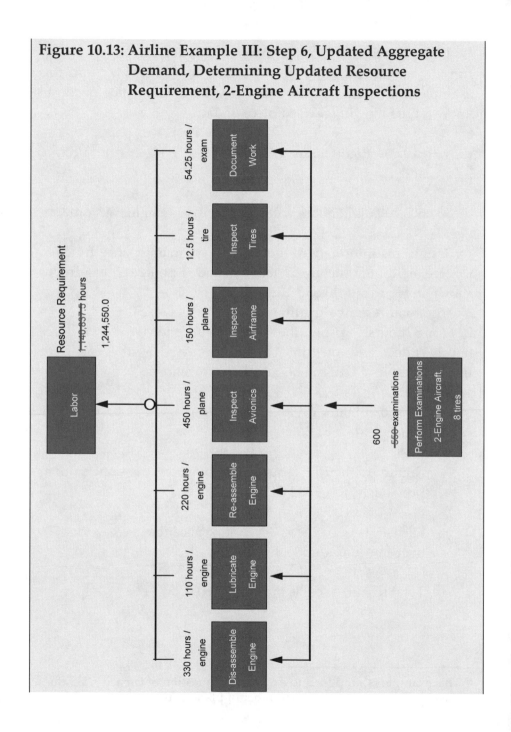

Figure 10.13: Airline Example III: Step 6, Updated Aggregate Demand, Determining Updated Resource Requirement, 2-Engine Aircraft Inspections

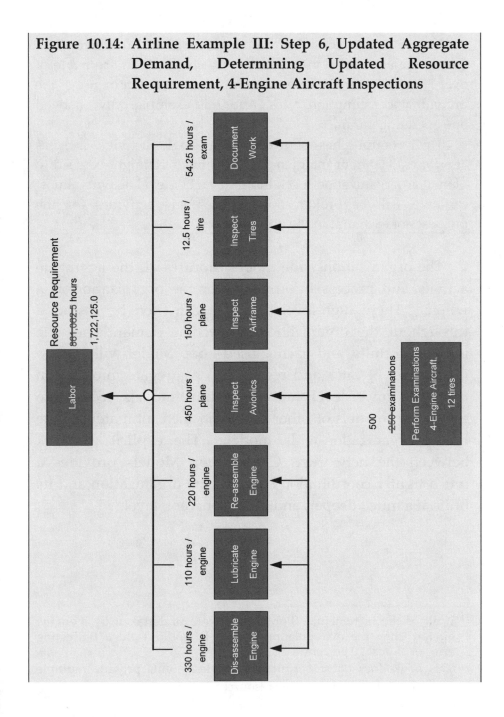

Figure 10.14: Airline Example III: Step 6, Updated Aggregate Demand, Determining Updated Resource Requirement, 4-Engine Aircraft Inspections

Note that the recalculated amount is $8,550,000 greater than the simple extrapolation approach initially used, an error rate of over 7.5%. This error is due to not recognizing the influence of the individual consumption rates. And this example only changed one operating parameter![61]

This example has shown that a single activity such as "perform 1,000 hour maintenance examination" might be used to plan at an organization level, but that higher level activity almost certainly will be broken down into many activities for the purposes of each unit in the organization.

The organization-wide model captures all the aggregate activity and process information for the organization as a whole. These high-level activities can then be cascaded throughout the organization to become demands for the individual units, and each Closed-Loop Model will contain its own set of rates and resources. Aggregate information from the lower-level individual unit models feeds into networked models of other units and then ultimately to the linked organization-wide model. The explicit feedback between the networked Closed-Loop Models provides a much tighter coordination between the organization and its units at a much deeper, and more coherent, level.[62]

---

[61] If all of the incremental flight hours were undertaken by 4-engine aircraft, then the extrapolation approach would yield a budgeting error of almost 10 percent.

[62] This book does not cover situations where units provide multiple services with interchangeable resources.

10.4 UNDERSTANDING THE RELATIONSHIP BETWEEN THE CLOSED-LOOP MODEL'S FINANCIAL RESULTS AND CASH FLOWS

To this point, the discussion has not differentiated between the accounting cost of resources provided, the cash outflows required to obtain and sustain those resources, and the requirements of Generally Accepted Accounting Principles (GAAP). The Closed-Loop Model implicitly uses a form of accrual accounting, whereby revenues and expenses are defined using the activity, resource, demand, and revenue elements of the model. With this method, there are two accounting issues to be aware of:

- The financial accounting definitions of revenues and expenses may not match those of the Closed-Loop Model. This may be an important issue if unit profits are calculated using GAAP and if managers are paid bonuses according to GAAP profits.

- Cash planning requires additional information on the size and timing of cash inflows and outflows, because accruals almost always differ from cash flows. The accruals can capture when the resources are used, but they can not capture when the resources are paid for.

The financial accounting and cash planning processes are linked to the Closed-Loop Model, but need to be run in parallel to generate coherent results.

Now that we have examined the building blocks in detail,
the next chapter addresses the issues of collecting the data
and building the systems architecture.

11 CHAPTER

The Architecture of an ABPB System

The previous chapters described the work required to establish and sustain the ABPB Process. This chapter builds upon the prior work and discusses the important final piece of the ABPB Process -- the ABPB System Architecture, as it relates specifically to feeding each individual Closed-Loop Model and the organization's network of such models. The architecture is the design for all of the major tools, data sources, and linkages required to develop and sustain the ABPB Process through each Closed-Loop Model.

The ABPB System Architecture defines the data and structure required to implement, support, and maintain the Closed-Loop Models. Data from a variety of sources such as the general ledger and its sub-ledgers, operational systems, planning systems, and manual and "what-if" sources are required to maintain the network of Closed-Loop Models. A strong data management system is a necessary condition for turning the Closed-Loop Models into the self-sustaining ABPB Process.

In today's environment, information technology, data warehouse tools, and activity-based software have reached the point where enterprise-wide Activity-Based Information Systems (ABIS) are practical to implement. An ABIS is the infrastructure and contents that hold the data required by an activity-based process and/or system. The ABIS may include technology such as specialized, customized, or off-the-shelf software, as well as manual approaches and/or solutions. Figure 11.1 illustrates a typical ABPB System Architecture. Systems development will follow the ABPB Implementation Program that was shown in Figure 5.1. Initial data collection and population of a Closed-Loop Model will involve considerable manual effort. However, as the ABPB Process matures, a robust and automated infrastructure of data collection, transformation, storage, model population, and reporting tools should be implemented to successfully sustain the ABPB Process.

11.1 DATA SOURCES

As pilot ABPB Projects succeed and full implementation begins, the need for good data and robust data management become critical aspects of implementing a successful and sustainable ABPB Process. To support the process, the data should be organized to easily provide planning and/or budget analysts a historical picture of each of the Closed-Loop Model variables (demand, consumption rates, resource capacity, unit cost, and product/service price) so that "what-if" scenarios can be analyzed based on past and planned performance. Demand estimates should be grounded in meaningful prediction algorithms, whose *assumptions* require periodic validation (see the discussion in Chapter 10). Consumption rates, if each remains within an agreed-upon range, can continue to be used without modification.

Figure 11.1: The ABPB System Architecture

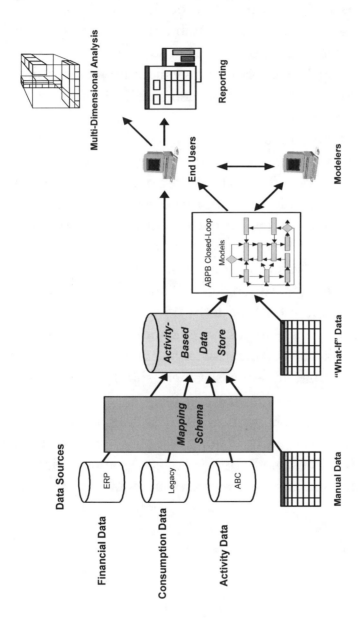

Adapted from PCS Consulting Inc.

Except for major reorganizations, staffing changes, and capital transactions (all of which are quantifiable), resource capacity will remain relatively stable from period to period. Thus, the focus of data collection in support of ongoing use of Closed-Loop Models is one of validating existing model data and changing only those elements that move outside established limits.

The predictive nature of the Closed-Loop Models being constructed or maintained requires a unique emphasis on the data collection effort. There are many data collection mechanisms available to support the creation and updating of a Closed-Loop Model. In early pilot development, many of these tools will be executed manually. However, as the ABPB Implementation Program matures and the sustaining processes are institutionalized, automated means of collection or validation need to be developed. The challenge is often data quality, such as non-standard entries, missing elements, multiple but inconsistent data sources, or simply incorrect information. An assessment should be made early in the system design as to the integrity, accuracy, consistency, and availability of data across all of the organization's key information systems. The following discussion outlines methods for collecting model data and some of the sources where such data may be found, as shown in Figure 11.2.

Figure 11.2: Typical Sources of Data for a Closed-Loop Model

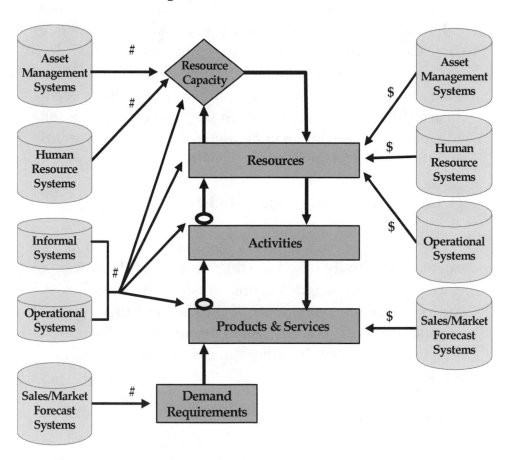

11.1.1 Existing Enterprise and/or Legacy Systems

There are significant amounts of data in most organizations' legacy and enterprise systems. A major challenge for the ABPB Implementation Program is getting access to this data quickly and consistently.

It is likely that much of the required financial data, and some of the operational and plan data, resides in separate on-line transaction processing (OLTP) databases. These databases may be part of an integrated enterprise system or consist of multiple legacy systems. The ABPB System does not require a transactional level of detail. Often the transaction detail must be summarized before being incorporated into the ABPB System, and this has the advantage of reducing the volume of data actually entering into the ABPB System.

11.1.2 Activity-Based Costing Models

As discussed in Chapter 1, Section 1.5, ABPB is not calculating Activity-Based Costing in reverse. However, an existing Activity-Based Costing model can serve as the source for some components of ABPB. The definitions of products/services, activities, and resources can be used to establish these key building blocks of the Closed-Loop Model.

11.1.3 Interviews

Interviews are useful when a limited number of subject matter experts can provide valid data. For example, knowledge experts can frequently provide operational consumption rates that are very close to what would be derived if the detailed data were systemically collected. In this way, sufficiently precise consumption rates can be used without the added cost of collecting the data on an ongoing basis.   These knowledge experts can also provide periodic validation of existing consumption rates as the Closed-Loop Model is updated over time.   Interviews can be conducted with one person at a time or in small groups, the latter being particularly useful in organizational cultures where open discussion and possibly disagreement is fostered, and thus may lead to better results.

11.1.4 Surveys

Surveys used to collect resource and activity metrics (such as percentages of time) for use in Activity-Based Costing models are generally inappropriate for use in an ABPB environment.   This is because ABPB is focused on future effort required rather than past distribution of time. Surveys can be designed to develop demand projections or inputs for consumption rates, and they can provide a valuable source of required inputs in a data-poor environment.   They can also be used to obtain workforce buy-in or for validating the predictive results of the Closed-Loop Models.

11.1.5 Sampling

Sampling is useful for quick analysis, or when automated data is unavailable in useful form.   Similar to capturing consumption rates from knowledge experts, sampling can capture performance for a specific period of time.   This data can then be extrapolated for use in the Closed-Loop Model to represent the total time period or to estimate consumption rates for multiple activities or resources. This method also produces results of adequate precision with much less effort than that required to implement an ongoing data collection system. However, sampling and extrapolation both have practical limits and these must be considered for each data element of the Closed-Loop Model.

11.1.6 Time Studies

These approaches are well suited to cases where detailed analysis is desired in order to reduce data integrity concerns for consumption rate calculations and increase the credibility of results. Scientific methods such as "Time and Motion" studies and "Discrete Simulation Modeling" can be used to great advantage for establishing control and modeling the probabilities of outcomes. The range of time study analysis can vary from counting activities and tracking time to using industrial engineering time and motion study methods.

11.1.7 The Optimal Level of Detail

With any of the techniques discussed, care should be taken to ensure that the data collection cost is worth the additional precision provided through a more detailed, and costly, collection method. Figure 11.3 illustrates a view of how the cost of data collection and maintenance can grow significantly in an attempt to reduce the cost of error in the model or results.

Figure 11.3: The Optimal Level of Detail in the ABPB System

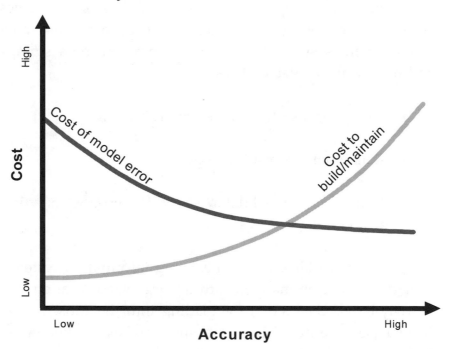

As shown, a point is reached when the cost of obtaining increased accuracy (i.e. reduced cost of model error) is exceeded by the cost of obtaining the required data and maintaining the model. In other words, there are diminishing returns from increased data accuracy.

11.2 THE ACTIVITY-BASED DATA STORE

Much of the data in its raw form may be ill-suited for direct input into the Closed-Loop Model. Typically, data is incomplete or inconsistent and thus requires transformation, cleansing, and/or summarization prior to use. This data needs a storage location, whether it is a formal data-mart, data warehouse, or a series of specific folders or directories in an information system. To develop an enterprise data management system, three different types of data storage technology are available. These are:

- On-line transaction processing (OLTP) ,

- Relational data warehouses, and

- Multi-dimensional databases and/or on-line analytical processing (OLAP) systems.

To use available data from existing information systems, that data must be mapped into an organized location, the activity-based data store, for loading into the Closed-Loop Model (see Figure 11.1). One such process is known as Extract, Transform, and Load, which takes data from its raw form and organizes, validates, and cleans the data before loading it into the data store. Sometimes this process has already been accomplished in existing data warehouses or data-marts. The activity-based data store provides a dedicated place for holding transformed data ready for use.

11.3 REPORTING AND ANALYSIS

The activity-based data store can also serve as the data source for activity-based reporting and analysis. Reports can be provided to various end-users showing their plan and budget projections as well as an ongoing evaluation of actual versus plan results. In addition to holding aggregate plan data for the Closed-Loop Models, the data store may also be the location used to hold historical data for Activity-Based Costing models and aggregated actual data for actual to plan reporting.

One of the technologies used for deploying planning and budgeting results is on-line analytical processing (OLAP), also known as "multi-dimensional" reporting. The multi-dimensional nature of OLAP is ideal for analyzing settings where there may be many dimensions, such as sales offices, customers, plants, processes, and/or markets, countries, time periods, etc.

11.4 THE APBP DATA MANAGEMENT SYSTEM

Sustaining the ABPB System Architecture is dependent on maintaining the ABPB Data Management System. Thoughtful planning and sound documentation are required in order to build and maintain such a system. Included should be the elements of system architecture, data collection, data storage and transformation, and reporting and analysis. A description of the system architecture (e.g. hardware, software, and interfaces) and data elements, along with departmental roles and responsibilities, should be clearly documented.

Whether automated or manual data collection is used, one of the most important things is to identify the best available data source and to *document* the method so that it is repeatable over time.   Included in the data element documentation should be data sources, business rules, assumptions and methods for deriving the data, and parties responsible for providing updates and maintaining the data.

For certain data elements, the ideal data may not be available. In this case, the organization should start with a reasonable surrogate and again document the reasons why the ideal data is not available, what could or should be done to make it available, and why the surrogate is reasonable. Ideally, an organization should identify those data elements and factors with the largest potential impact on model results, and prioritize these in a comprehensive data collection improvement plan. Over time, these weaknesses should be assessed, challenged, validated, calibrated, and improved upon.

As the organization develops the internal discipline inherent in the collection, storage, reporting, and documentation methods outlined here, the quality of the resulting information will be reflected in how the Closed Loop Models' predicted outcomes align with achieved results. This improved quality, in turn, will enhance the credibility of the ABPB Process as a planning and budgeting methodology and help foster the adoption of ABPB in other areas of the organization.

This chapter completes the second part of the book, the discussion of how to implement the ABPB Process in an organization. The discussion has gone from planning the initial pilot, through building the first Closed-Loop Model, sustaining the model, and expanding the ABPB Process throughout the organization.

The final part of this book, Part 3, shows how the ABPB Process interacts with the other business processes inside the organization.

PART 3

DERIVING VALUE FROM THE ACTIVITY-BASED PLANNING AND BUDGETING PROCESS

12 CHAPTER

Integrating the ABPB Process with the Traditional Budgeting Process

12.1 AN OVERVIEW OF PART 3

Now that we have described how the organization expands the Closed-Loop Models into the self-sustaining ABPB Process, the final part of this book turns to how the ABPB Process can be successfully integrated with other important management processes. Chapter 12 discusses how the new ABPB Process used in some units can peacefully co-exist with the traditional budgeting process used in other units, while Chapter 13 describes how the ABPB Process can be integrated with other Strategic Management Initiatives such as the Balanced Scorecard and Six Sigma. Chapter 14 summarizes the book and the ABPB Group's key findings.

Using the ABPB Process does not mean abandoning traditional budgeting methods altogether, and the remainder of this chapter describes how the ABPB Process can be integrated with traditional budgeting practices.

12.2 TRADITIONAL BUDGETING PROCESSES

Traditional budgeting processes usually are defined in terms of general ledger accounts and involve setting budgets based on organizational structures. Traditional budgets focus on functions, not activities and processes, and on costs not quality or time. As a result, a traditional budget centers on resource cost by function, rather than on the demand for outputs and the requirements placed on activities and resources. Traditional budgets also tend to be driven from what each functional group spent in the prior period, plus or minus some percentage that is mandated from the central budget administration, without adequate consideration of customer or resource requirements, as shown in Figure 12.1.

Figure 12.1: Traditional Budgeting

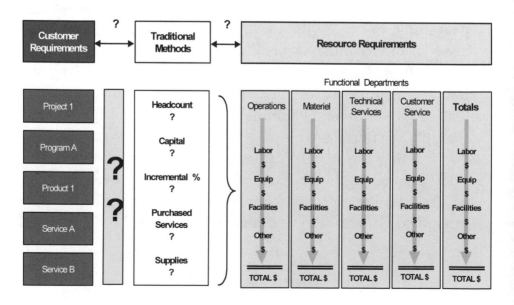

Traditional budgeting does not identify the cause and effect relationships of outputs, activities, and resources. There are certainly functions within organizations where these relationships do not exist or are very difficult to capture. For these functions, or for functions that comprise a very small part of the overall cost or output of the organization, traditional budgeting methods may be adequate and appropriate.

12.3 THE NECESSITY OF CO-EXISTENCE

An ABPB Process can co-exist effectively with traditional budgeting processes. The best of both approaches and tools can be used and integrated to create the Formal Budget. No matter how "pure" an activity-based budgeting manager wishes to be, certain types of expenses will not have an apparent or useable causal relationship with demands for products or services. These expenses probably should be budgeted using traditional methods.

Every organization and organizational unit should use the tool that is most appropriate for its individual planning and budgeting requirements. Three situations should be considered for each organizational unit, in the following sequence:

1. Does the unit have identifiable and well-defined cost objects, business processes, and activities? If not, can they be defined? If both of these questions are answered in the negative, then implementing the ABPB Process may not be possible.

2. Are most of a unit's costs causally related to some form of cost object, be it a product, service, or customer?   If not, then implementing the ABPB Process may not be possible.

3. If there is a solid causal relationship from definable processes to defined cost objects, then implementing the ABPB process may be a good choice.   However, the question of costs and benefits remains. Organizational units that comprise an insignificant percentage of the total cost of the organization may find that the benefits of using the ABPB Process are outweighed by the costs.   As such, the transition to the ABPB Process may not be economically beneficial. However, this economic assessment must be made relative to the costs and benefits of the traditional budgeting process.

Implementing an ABPB Process is not necessarily feasible or appropriate for all units within an organization. While it seems logical to connect resources with cost objects in all parts of an organization, such links may not be practical or economically worthwhile in every situation.

12.4 TRANSITION AND EXPANSION

As with Activity-Based Cost Management, incorporating the ABPB Process into the planning and budgeting framework of an organization is an iterative process. The organization must not only *believe in the process* but must also *believe the results* it generates.   That belief only comes through consistent use and refinement of the structure and data that comprise the Closed-Loop Model within a given organization.

Chapter 5 introduced the ABPB Implementation Program, shown again in Figure 12.2, to illustrate the overall implementation cycle within an organization.

The figure shows the familiar pilot then expansion sequence, along with the iterative nature of activity-based implementations of any kind.   When the ABPB Process is deployed in the manner outlined in Part 2 of this book, the organization will create the necessary confidence in the reliability of the calculated resource requirements coming from the Closed-Loop Model.   Eventually, the organization can transition from managing unit-level ABPB Projects to managing the organization-wide ABPB Process.

Once the concepts of the Closed-Loop Model and the ABPB Process have been proven by the project pilot, these experiences can be leveraged to the iterative expansion of ABPB into other units.   The experience gained during the project pilot both improves the chances for success of the ABPB Projects in other units and shortens the time required for implementation in those units.

Not every area of the organization will be ready for transition to the ABPB Process at the same time.   Some units may switch or transition before others, while some may never adopt the ABPB Process. The expansion of the ABPB Process is shown in Figure 12.3.

Figure 12.2: The ABPB Implementation Program

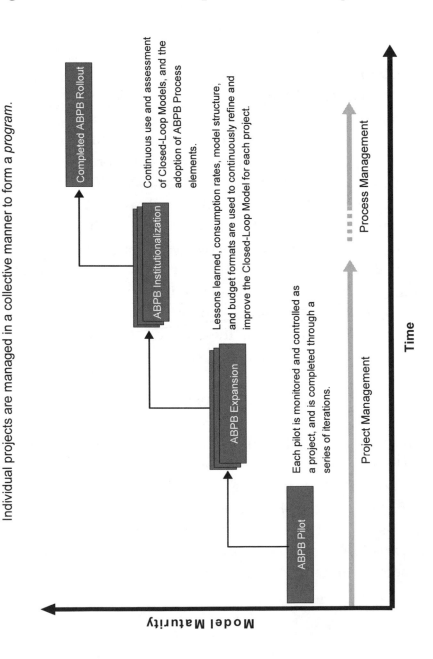

Figure 12.3: The Spread of the ABPB Process

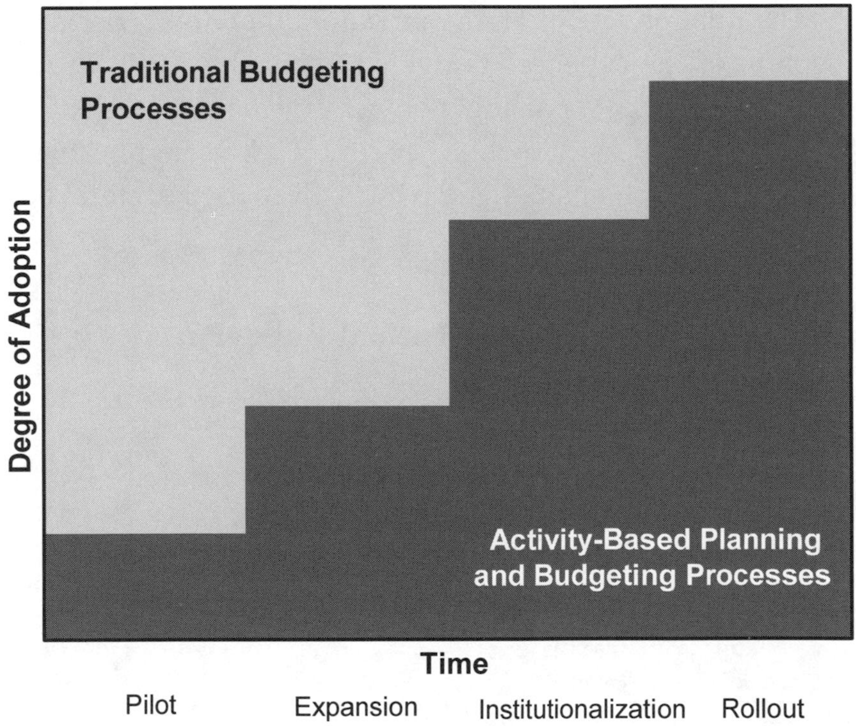

Traditional Budgeting Processes

Activity-Based Planning and Budgeting Processes

Degree of Adoption

Time

Pilot   Expansion   Institutionalization   Rollout

An integrated effort is one that has the common goal of improving the organization as a whole. Such an effort can create a budget that articulates the needs of the entire organization and a budget process that recognizes the strengths and limitations of both traditional methods and the ABPB Process. To integrate traditional and new processes effectively, the organization must acknowledge where the ABPB Process adds value and where it does not.

12.5 THE FINAL, FORMAL BUDGET

The total budget of an organization, therefore, consists of the sum of the expenses budgeted using the ABPB Process and those budgeted using non-activity based approaches. This approach, as shown in Figure 12.4, is applicable to organizations of all sizes and across all market sectors, both public and private.

Figure 12.4: Creating the Formal Budget

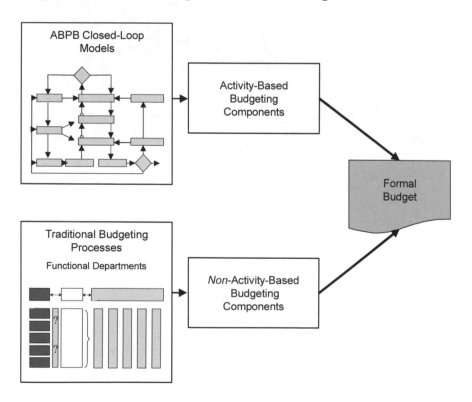

12.6 CASH FLOW

Cash is the lifeblood of an organization, and forecasting cash flow is an important part of the planning process. A budget prepared using the ABPB Process is principally a cash requirements document. The Closed-Loop Model develops plans for physical and financial requirements of the organization. These detailed plans provide a blueprint for when and where the organization needs resources. However, identifying the precise quantities of cash required at appropriate times is equally important, and usually requires tools and methods specifically designed to meet that objective. These cash requirements must be matched to cash availability.

12.7 SUMMARY

An organization needs to determine which of its units are candidates to implement the ABPB Process, initially and over time, and which should continue to use traditional planning and budgeting methods. The broad considerations for deciding whether an organizational unit is an appropriate candidate for adopting an ABPB Process include its relative size, the definability of its cost objects and processes, and a cost-benefit analysis.

After decisions are made as to which units should plan and budget using the Closed-Loop Model, and those efforts are completed, creating the formal budget becomes a relatively mechanical exercise. Over time, as additional units transition to the Closed-Loop Model, they have the assurance that the framework to incorporate their results into the budget is in place.

The traditional budgeting process is not the only situation where there are synergies with the ABPB Process.
The next chapter discusses how the ABPB Process can integrate with other important strategic initiatives.

13 CHAPTER

Integrating the ABPB Process with other Strategic Management Initiatives

In today's dynamic business climate, there are many management initiatives that executives need to consider in order to lead their organizations towards world-class or leading-edge performance. CAM-I believes that a "best practice" approach should be used to implement these initiatives in a synergistic and integrated manner.

Recognizing the need for an integrated approach to cost and performance, CAM-I developed the Strategic Management Process (SMP) Model (McNair et al. 2000). The CAM-I SMP Model provides a logical framework to understand the critical high-level decisions an organization must make and the information required for these decisions. Figure 13.1 presents the SMP Model, adapted slightly to reflect the inclusion of Activity-Based Planning and Budgeting.

The SMP Model views every organization as having four basic decision domains, the key elements of strategy, that must be set and reviewed periodically:

- Customers/markets (why an organization is in business),

Figure 13.1: Integrating Strategic Management Processes

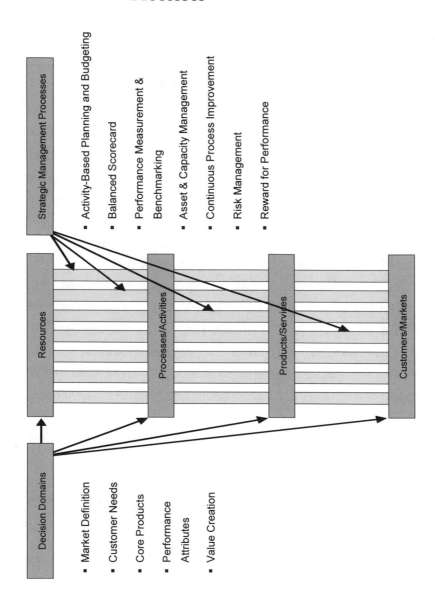

Source: Adapted from McNair et. al. (2000)

- Products/services (what is delivered to customers),

- Processes/activities (how products/services will be provided), and

- Resources (how much is needed to provide products/services).

Strategic Management Processes, such as ABPB and the Balanced Scorecard, cut across and link the decision domains. An important aspect of each SMP is that it coordinates the decisions across the domains and throughout the organization. Just as it is important that each SMP provide a coherent connection to each domain, it is equally important that each SMP be coordinated with each of the others. Synchronized actions and results, so critical to the success of the global enterprise, cannot be achieved through the use of fragmented information systems or disjointed tools and techniques: integration and coordination are required.

Implementing a systemic performance management system within a holistic framework of common metrics can provide clarity and focus for all employees in terms of strategy communication and execution (The Office of Management and Budget 2002). The ABPB Process incorporates performance management concepts that link and improve cross-functional performance with the strategic goals and objectives of the organization. By adopting and implementing the ABPB Process, organizations will not only add value to their planning and budgeting processes, but will also achieve measurable improvements to their overall strategic management systems.   Data integration, target setting, and performance reporting will all be executed in a more consistent and focused manner.

In particular, it is important to understand that the ABPB Process is a management tool and should not be viewed in isolation. As Henry Morris stated: [63]

> Budgeting and planning are not new applications, but are attracting renewed interest in the light of volatile business conditions.   The need to tie budgeting and planning to business performance management signals the gradual decline of standalone applications for these processes.

This chapter discusses how integrating the ABPB Process with other key strategic management processes can add significant value to the organization.

13.1 BALANCED SCORECARD

The starting point for the ABPB Process is the development of an organizational strategy. Thus, the ABPB Process links directly to the core rationale of the Balanced Scorecard – strategy execution (Kaplan and Norton 2001). The ABPB Process creates a planning discipline and feedback mechanism that is directly linked to an

---

[63] Morris, H. 2002. *Budgeting, Planning, and the Three Levels of Analytic Applications.* IDC Research Document #28068, Abstract.

organization's strategy.   Budgeting by activities allows planning to better follow strategy.

Linking the ABPB Process with the Balanced Scorecard helps to promote an operational *and* financial view of planning and budgeting. An organization can then focus on the planning component rather than just the financial budgeting aspect.   This focus represents an underlying theme of this book, that more emphasis should be placed on planning and less on detailed line-item budgeting.   The resulting employee and organizational alignment ensures balance in the overall ABPB Process.

The Closed-Loop Model promotes an understanding of the relationships between various operational metrics, some of which can be identified as leading indicators, and ultimately their impact on financial metrics, which are clearly lagging indicators.   The "cause and effect" relationships between performance and cost can be understood using the Closed-Loop Model. Many of the elements that form a Closed-Loop Model (e.g. consumption rates, capacity utilization levels, and unit costs) can be identified as key performance indicators (KPIs).   By understanding how operational metrics drive financial results, management can assess which metrics generated the desired results, and therefore which should be used in the Balanced Scorecard.

A weakness of Balanced Scorecard implementations is the lack of connectivity to budgets or the understanding of what it costs to execute various competing strategic objectives. Linking the Balanced Scorecard with the Closed-Loop Model helps to eliminate this weakness. For example, when a Balanced Scorecard initiative identifies performance that is failing to meet strategic objectives, process improvements are often recommended to close the gap between actual and target performance; but the resource implications of such initiatives are rarely considered in assessing these initiatives. Because the Closed-Loop Model is predictive in nature, the resources required to meet these improvements and close the gap can be identified. Thus, the Closed-Loop Model becomes a valuable tool for assessing priorities and the cost of process changes, creating a more predictive capability in evaluating the expected impact of scorecard-driven initiatives.

One of the limitations of the traditional budgeting process is that it creates a fixed performance target which inhibits the ability of the Balanced Scorecard to drive strategic initiatives. The use of a dynamic budgeting approach, such as the Closed-Loop Model, helps to break this fixed linkage and thus aids the Balanced Scorecard in achieving its intended purpose.

13.2 PERFORMANCE MEASUREMENT AND BENCHMARKING

Linking performance measurement and benchmarking to the overall ABPB Process establishes a cohesive framework for standardizing planning and measurement throughout an organization. This framework is consistent with the CAM-I definition of Activity-Based Cost Management (White 1997).

Benchmarking is generally applied to establish "best practices", and can be undertaken internally within the organization and/or externally with other organizations. As applied in the context of ABPB, the benefits of measuring performance and benchmarking can be summarized as follows:

- Operational consumption rates and the resulting cost information developed in a Closed-Loop Model can be used as points of comparison and to suggest areas of improvement. Applying these benchmark rates across multiple units in an organization provides a superior opportunity to compare practices, leverage knowledge and learning, and measure improvements.

- Trend analysis of key performance measures and their relative performance against benchmarks can be assessed and progress evaluated. These trends allow for the assessment of changes in consumption rates within and across organizational units.

- Output and outcome target setting can be assessed more appropriately by comparing targets across units and benchmarking the impact of changes in consumption rates across units.

- Elements of the Closed-Loop Model are linked and can help create a more balanced approach to performance measurement thus avoiding the pitfalls of measures that are solely tied to traditional financial budgets.

Performance measurement and benchmarking are critical Strategic Management Processes. Selecting appropriate KPIs for these purposes can be greatly assisted by linking to the key operational measures that drive the Closed-Loop Model. These links support the adage of "measures motivate" and are highly relevant in today's business culture.

13.3 ASSET AND CAPACITY MANAGEMENT

Capacity is a key element in the Closed-Loop Model and provides a clear link with asset and capacity management initiatives. The Closed-Loop Model follows and supports CAM-I's view of capacity (Klammer 1996), namely that capacity is measured at the resource level.[64] Understanding resource utilization in terms of operational balance can help with capacity optimization, including the recognition and reduction of idle capacity and make/buy decision analysis. A more dynamic planning process creates an awareness of the effect of variability, such as changes in forecasts or seasonality issues, on resource requirements, and the ensuing financial budget implications. In addition, the Closed-Loop Model can provide a link with Economic Value Added (EVA®) and other return-based approaches, thereby optimizing resource consumption and providing a different view of financial results that is more suitable for management decision-making.

---

[64] As was noted earlier in this book, it can also be argued that activities and processes have capacity. At one level this is true, but ultimately activity and process capacity is provided by resources.

13.4 CONTINUOUS PROCESS IMPROVEMENT (INCLUDING SIX SIGMA)

The activity consumption rates used in the Closed-Loop Model can be used on a "what-if" basis to focus on continuous process improvement, through approaches such as Six Sigma. Sensitivity analysis of these rates can provide an understanding of "cause and effect" relationships and subsequently offers assistance in prioritizing improvement efforts (discussed in Chapter 8).   The link between improvements in consumption rates and the subsequent creation or freeing up of capacity is highly visible in the Closed-Loop Model.

The Six Sigma movement continues to grow and there are many well-known advocates and success stories associated with its implementation. Companies operating between three and four sigma (the norm) typically spend about 25 percent of their revenues fixing problems or errors; implementing Six Sigma can get this down to less than 1 percent (Harry and Schroeder 2000, 15).   Jack Welch of General Electric reported the following:[65]

By 1998, we had generated $750 million Six Sigma savings over and above our investment and would get $1.5 billion the next year.

Savings of this magnitude can be budgeted for using an activity-based approach. The Closed-Loop Model can show

---

[65] Welch, J. and J. Byrne. 2001. *Jack: Straight From The Gut*. New York, NY: Warner Business Books, 335.

the potential financial gains of ongoing improvements relating to quality metrics when the costs of defects are taken into consideration. For example, an organization might use the Closed-Loop Model to measure the difference in activity and resource requirements of, say, warranty service at varying levels of sigma performance.

13.5 RISK MANAGEMENT

The Closed-Loop Model allows different scenarios to be developed in a consistent manner to help evaluate predictable aspects of risk. Managers can review the impact that their planning assumptions have on the key performance metrics of their organization and can study alternatives to avoid or mitigate "worst case" situations. Because the Closed-Loop Model is not constrained to an annual time period, organizations that use the ABPB Process can reduce risk by promoting more frequent reviews of the operational and financial planning process, leading to earlier awareness of potential risk issues.

As discussed in Chapter 4, military organizations can use the Closed-Loop Model to establish resource requirements to meet specific levels of readiness. Risk management is becoming an important element of this readiness assessment and an area where future research and development is likely to take place.

13.6 REWARD FOR PERFORMANCE

Incentive compensation systems, monetary or otherwise, should differentiate between group and individual rewards. For example, one approach might consist of a 3-tier reward system based on:

- Overall company performance *in relative terms* - how well did the organization perform with respect to its competitors or benchmarks (e.g. market share),

- Team results - how well did the team perform against *specific targets* (e.g. meeting production quotas or process improvement initiatives), and

- Individual accomplishments - how well did the individual respond to particular *learning objectives* (e.g. updating professional skills).

The ABPB Process can help to provide a more realistic link to the reward system in terms of team performance. With an effective ABPB Process, rewards for performance can be linked to both operational and financial results, especially if the performance measures have been linked through Balanced Scorecard initiatives. Rewarding excellent performance can help an organization avoid the gaming that can occur when compensation is linked to the traditional budgeting process only using financial results. With an ABPB Process, a more focused, team approach to achieving organizational success can be fostered.

This book has now gone full circle, from defining the Closed-Loop Model to providing a project planning and implementation methodology, and finally to showing how the ABPB Process can be linked with other strategic management initiatives. Integration with other processes can best be achieved by following a holistic framework, where common metrics are used and shared across the various initiatives.

The final chapter of this book summarizes the results and provides conclusions.

14 CHAPTER

Summary and Conclusions

The budgeting process may be the most critical and yet most maligned process in any organization. On the positive side, the budgeting process is usually the only management process that is required to completely integrate information from all units of the organization, and thus is the unique document that ties together all units of the organization. The budget allocates resources, aids in operational planning, serves as a basis for performance evaluation, and performs many other functions.

Yet in spite of its central role, current budgeting practice has many flaws. The traditional budgeting process:

- Is too time consuming,

- Requires too many iterations,

- Can be very costly,

- Does not address capacity,

- Is based on an extrapolation of prior periods' data,

- Is influenced by political gaming, and

- Receives limited buy-in or acceptance of results.

The recent spate of corporate malfeasance is partially attributable to traditional budgeting, since the pressure to demonstrate revenue growth in the private sector is often exerted through the budgeting process.

There is a clear need for change. Some advocate "blowing up the budget" (Hope and Fraser 2003). But we believe that most organizations retain a need for time-period specific plans and budgets, to act as target-setting, monitoring, controlling, and measuring tools. *Thus, the issue is not whether, but how, to budget.*

This book shows the way. The ABPB Process uses activity-based logic to generate a more detailed and rational model of an organization's activity and resource relationships. It solves many of the problems of the traditional budgeting process and simultaneously expands the potential usefulness of the final results. Elements of the Closed-Loop Model and the ABPB Process have been implemented by many of the authors of this book in multiple sectors of the economy, including transportation, consumer products, utilities, manufacturing, shared services, the military, and in a branch of the United States Department of Justice. The Closed-Loop Model and the ABPB Process are the most significant development in the field of Planning and Budgeting in the last thirty years.

14.1 BENEFITS OF THE ABPB PROCESS

Throughout this book, we have presented the ABPB Process and its underlying calculation engine, the Closed-Loop Model. A comprehensive list of the major benefits follows. We have split the list up into benefits to the planning and budgeting process and benefits to other related management processes.

14.1.1 Benefits to the Planning and Budgeting Process

1. *Reduction in the time and cost of generating a budget.* Because the Closed-Loop Model first obtains an operational balance, then a financial balance, it can reduce the time and cost of generating a budget. In particular, it can remove the needless steps of calculating the financial effect of operationally infeasible plans.

2. *More accurate costs and better decision-making.* The use of an explicit model relating demands, activities, and resources allows the organization to improve its operational and financial plans by incorporating drivers and operating linkages not found in traditional budgeting approaches. This additional detail will result in improved budgets and thus better decision-making.

3. *More specific and cohesive link with the strategic plan.* The use of the causal logic embedded in the Closed-

Loop Model allows the financial effects of the strategic plan to be more precisely understood. The organization can address the issues of how the plan generates costs throughout the organization, including the secondary and tertiary effects on lower-level units.

4. *Added ability to adjust activity and resource consumption rates.* Activity and resource consumption rates are not collected in traditional budgeting systems. The Closed-Loop Model explicitly identifies them and provides management with knowledge necessary to control them.

5. *Additional methods to adjust capacity.* The addition of non-unit based levers to the budgeting system adds several new ways that the organization can balance resource capacity. The organization can draw on activity consumption rates, resource consumption rates, or both, as additional tools in order to balance resource supply and demand.

6. *Reduced time to collect information.* A more understandable and logical budgeting process should decrease both the cost and number of budget iterations by increasing the visibility of operating parameters and reducing the amount of time to gather information.

7. *Disagreements become more transparent.*   A model derived from actual operating relationships should assist in decreasing the amount of internal argument about activity and resource requirements and hence lower budgeting costs.

8. *Decrease in political gaming.* Because the Closed-Loop Model focuses on generating a budget explicitly from activities and resources, the scope for political gaming should decline.   The de-politicization of budgeting will almost certainly improve the integrity of the budget process.   And since the budget is likely to be used as a key input to performance measurement, an improved budget will also improve performance measurement and, in turn, the reporting of financial information.

9. *Easier to communicate and increased buy-in.* Because the budget can be reported in activity form, one that is generally better understood by operating managers and staff, it will be easier to communicate to all employees.   If the budget is better understood, buy-in is likely to increase.

10. *Improved understanding by managers.* By providing an understanding of how resources and activities are related, managers will have a better basis for taking action.

11. *Improved justification for budget requests.* Because the budget numbers are generated from a cause-and-effect model of the organization, it is easier to see the source of desired resource levels. Most arguments over budgets will now be recast into discussion over the future parameters of the Closed-Loop Model and away from the across-the-board percentage reduction philosophies of the past.

12. *Superior response to last minute changes in assumptions.* When assumptions change at the last minute, traditional budgeting processes tend to linearly extrapolate the latest results to generate a new budget. Since the individual units' Closed-Loop Models cascade demands and are networked, new assumptions will use the actual budgeting models to generate the new budgets. A last minute Closed-Loop Model budget will contain the same level of sophistication as a budget created without time pressure, and will be a significant improvement over the slap-dash fix applied under traditional budgeting.

13. *Improved cash forecasts.* The Closed-Loop Model generates a very detailed list of resource requirements. This list, in turn, can be used to generate a more detailed breakdown of cash requirements, and thereby improve cash forecasting.

14. *Improved "what-if" analysis.* The detailed resource and activity linkage at the heart of the Closed-Loop Model

provides a more analytical way to conduct "what-if" analysis. As suggested in Chapter 8, the potential impact of changing one or more levers can be quickly and visibly assessed.

14.1.2 Benefits to Other Management Processes

1. *Improved ability to tie together the budgeting process and the capacity management systems.* The explicit assessment of resource capacity in the Closed-Loop Model is not performed in traditional budgeting processes. This information can serve as the basis of an integrated budgeting and capacity management system.

2. *More rapid response to adjust capacity.* The early identification of capacity issues in the budgeting process gives the organization a longer lead time to balance capacity.

3. *More data that can be analyzed in greater depth.* The Closed-Loop Model provides detailed information about many more levels of the organization than just traditional product and customer profitability. Prime examples of this extra detail include analyses of resource capacities and utilization, operating performance metrics (i.e. consumption rates), and demand-activity-resource linkages.

4. *Improved performance evaluation system.* The linkage of resources and activities will lead to improved performance measures. In particular, the detailed information on capacity, activity consumption rates, and resource consumption rates may be useful in constructing improved performance measures.

5. *Improved comparisons of actual to forecast.* The Closed-Loop Model provides five levers to adjust the plan: demand quantities, consumption rates, resource capacities, resource unit costs, and product/service prices. Of these, consumption rates (both resource and activity) are new to budgeting, while resource capacity is greatly expanded upon. The use of expanded or new levers provides greater analytical capability to assess and predict results.

6. *Easier integration with other processes.* The Closed-Loop Model's explicit model of the organization will make it easier to integrate with other strategic management initiatives such as the Balanced Scorecard and Six Sigma, among others.

14.2 OUR UNDERLYING PHILOSOPHY AND THE PATH FORWARD

The CAM-I ABPB Group developed the ABPB Process and the Closed-Loop Model using a fairly straightforward philosophy. *The most important part of this philosophy is that budgeting is here to stay.* Existing budgeting processes are not working well, but there is a greater benefit to improving existing processes than in throwing out those processes and starting over.

One reason that traditional budgeting processes are failing is that other parts of the organization are starting to use more advanced techniques, leaving behind traditional budgets. An organization's cost management systems often use more sophisticated cost drivers, such as number and size of batches and assembly complexity, while its budgeting system still reflects a focus solely on fixed and variable costs. Another reason for dissatisfaction is that it most traditional budgeting   systems   are   disconnected   from   other management   processes   within   the   organization.   The approach in this book is to *fix the budget* by expanding several proven management techniques into the planning and budgeting area. The two critical elements of the ABPB Process are the extension of activity-based concepts and the expansion of the capacity system down to the activity and resource levels.

We have developed a planning and budgeting approach that extends activity-based logic into a new domain: planning and budgeting.   Activity-Based Planning and Budgeting is not Activity-Based Costing in reverse, although the two share many of the same building blocks. At the heart of this new approach is the Closed-Loop Model shown in Figure 14.1, which encapsulates an activity and resource consumption model of the organization. *Merely generating a model of this level of detail will alleviate many of the budgeting and planning problems inherent in most organizations.*

Figure 14.1: The CAM-I ABPB Closed-Loop Model

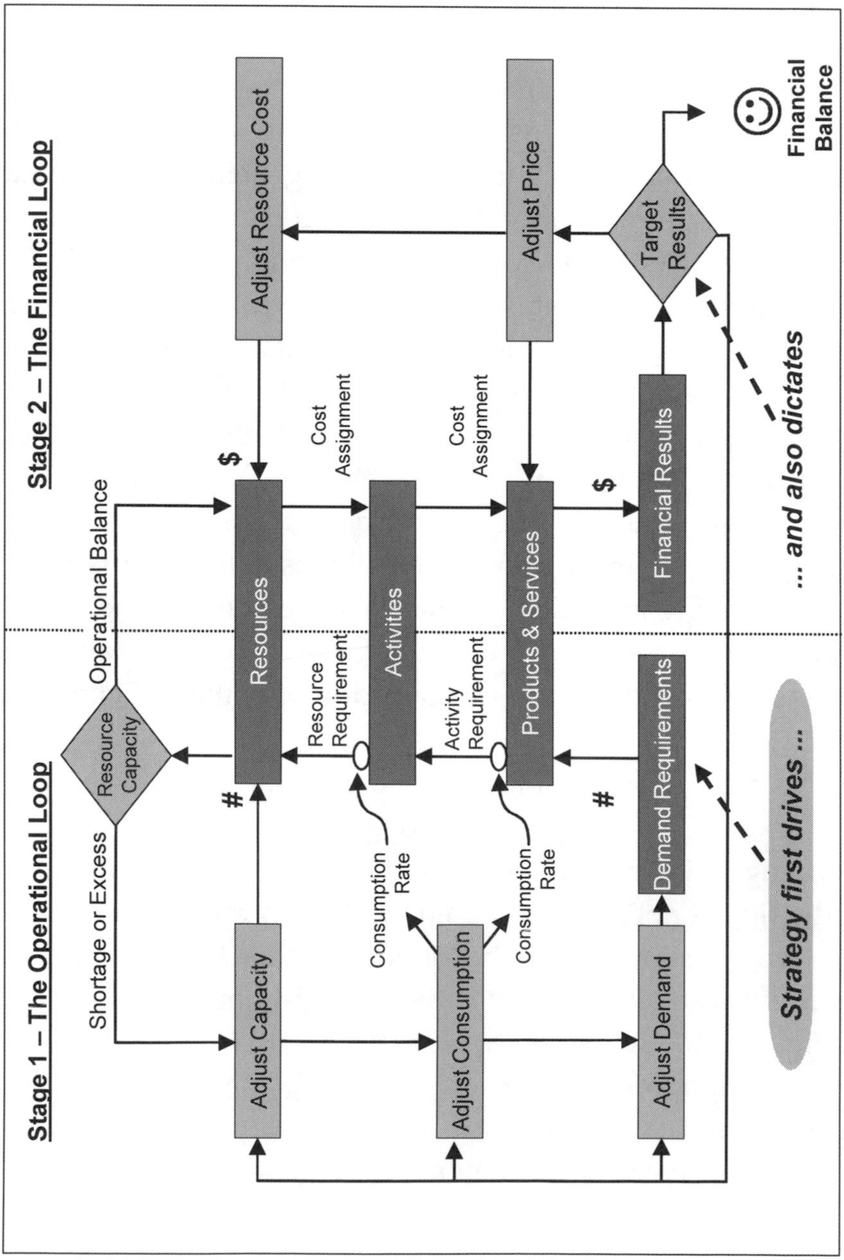

The Closed-Loop Model has two stages. The first, the operational loop, balances the demands on organizational resources and their supply in purely quantitative (but *non-financial*) terms. Generating the operational loop of the Closed-Loop Model can provide a huge impact for most organizations. Balancing resource demand and supply is the most difficult step in any plan and is valuable even without the inclusion of costs in the planning process.

The second stage, the financial loop, adds in the costs of resources and the value (i.e. revenue) of output to generate feasible financial plans. If the organization is in a stable environment, this step may be fairly easy to tackle. However, organizations with unstable resource costs or highly variable demand parameters will likely face much larger challenges than those in more stable environments. *It is important to remember that this problem is certainly no worse, and likely less severe, than what these organizations face without the Closed-Loop Model!*

If a Closed-Loop Model is built once and never updated, it will suffer a rapid death by having its output ignored. The second part of this book shows how to prevent this from occurring, by turning the initial Closed-Loop Model into the self-sustaining ABPB Process, shown in Figure 14.2. After performing the steps outlined in this figure, the organization will have a useful, self-generating planning and budgeting process.

We view the ABPB Process as having more to do with planning than with budgeting. The goal of the full process is to generate balanced *and* feasible operational and financial plans that will help many management processes, including

Figure 14.2: The CAM-I ABPB Process

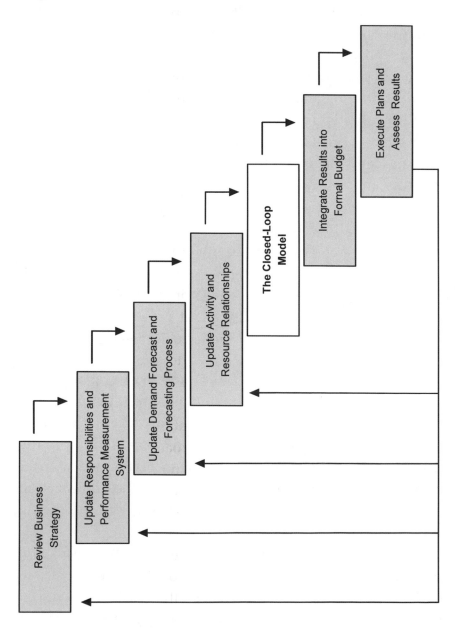

budgeting.   In the long run, a successful organization will switch from a primary focus on generating budgets to a more fruitful focus on planning, as shown in Figure 14.3.

We fully acknowledge that there are areas of the organization where an activity-based planning and budgeting approach may be inappropriate or uneconomical. In those settings, combining a budget from the Closed-Loop Model with one from a traditional process is straightforward and altogether supportive of the spirit and philosophy of this book.

There are always surprises when any new process is installed in an organization.   One possibility is that installing a more effective planning and budgeting process will lead to increased use of this more effective approach.   This may be a highly desirable state – imagine doing more of something users find valuable!   If management uses the Closed-Loop Model to run more business scenarios that was previously the case, then the number of budget iterations could actually increase.   But the benefits from each of these scenarios will far exceed the cost!

We also feel that if an organization uses an Activity-Based Planning and Budgeting approach, it will obtain the maximum benefit by restructuring the performance evaluation system to capture the new information revealed by the Closed-Loop Model. There are tremendous synergies in rewarding people using the same system as used to plan activities and allocate resources.   Since the activities forming the basis of this system are also the foundation of management's operating controls, all of the management systems can now be aligned.   The highest level of benefits

Figure 14.3: The Shift in the Relative Effort from Budgeting Towards Planning

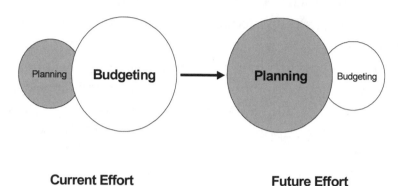

Current Effort   **Future Effort**

occurs if the organization restructures its performance evaluation system to follow the activity, process, and resource paths of the Closed-Loop Model.

A more realistic budget, one developed based on actual operating performance, will be viewed as having greater integrity than a traditional "get me 15% more" budget. We believe that increased integrity in the budgeting process will translate to a comparable increase in the integrity of the financial results that are reported against that budget.

This book has laid out a new approach for planning and budgeting, providing organizations with the basics of implementation as well as the principles and foundation elements required to sustain that approach.

The path has been lit ... it is now yours to follow.

A Glossary of Terms

Entries marked with an * are extracted from the CAM-I Glossary (Dierks and Cokins 2000).

Activity* Work performed by people, equipment, technologies, or facilities. Activities are usually described by the "action-verb-adjective-noun" grammar convention. Activities may occur in a linked sequence and activity-to-activity assignments may exist.

Activity Analysis* The process of identifying and cataloging activities for detailed understanding and documentation of their characteristics. An activity analysis is accomplished by means of interviews, group sessions, questionnaires, observations, and reviews of physical records of work.

Activity-Based Budgeting (ABB)* An approach to budgeting where a company uses an understanding of its activities and driver relationships to quantitatively estimate work load and resource requirements as part of an on-going business plan. Budgets show the types, number of, and cost of resources that activities are expected to consume, based on forecasted workloads. The budget is part of an organization's activity-based planning process and can be used in evaluating its success in setting and pursuing strategic goals (see also Activity-Based Planning).

Activity-Based Costing (ABC)* A methodology that measures the cost and performance of cost objects, activities, and resources. Cost objects consume activities and activities consume resources. Resource costs are assigned to activities based on their use of those resources, and activity costs are reassigned to cost objects (outputs) based on the cost objects' proportional use of those activities. Activity-based costing incorporates causal relationships between cost objects and activities and between activities and resources.

Activity-Based Information System (ABIS) The infrastructure and contents that hold the data required by an activity-based process and/or system. This may include technology such as specialized, customized, or off-the-shelf software, as well as manual approaches.

Activity-Based Management (ABM)* A discipline focusing on the management of activities within business processes as the route to continuously improve both the value received by customers and the profit earned in providing that value. ABM uses activity-based cost information and performance measurements to influence management action (see also Activity-Based Costing).

Activity–Based Planning (ABP)* Activity-based planning (ABP) is an ongoing process to determine activity and resource requirements (both financial and operational) based on the ongoing demand of products or services by specific customer needs. Resource requirements are compared to resources available and capacity issues are identified and managed. Activity-based budgeting (ABB) is based on the outputs of activity-based planning (see also Activity-Based Budgeting).

Activity-Based Planning and Budgeting Implementation Program A structured approach to introducing the Closed-Loop Model and Activity-Based Planning and Budgeting Process into an organization (see also Closed-Loop Model and Activity-Based Planning and Budgeting Process).

Activity-Based Planning and Budgeting Implementation Project The initial or subsequent implementation of the Activity-Based Planning and Budgeting Program in the form of a project. Each project is planned, executed, and controlled with a Closed-Loop Model as the deliverable (see also Closed-Loop Model and Activity-Based Planning and Budgeting Program).

Activity-Based Planning and Budgeting Process The business processes and techniques needed to sustain a unit's Closed-Loop Model over time (see also Closed-Loop Model).

Activity-Based Planning and Budgeting System Architecture The design of an Activity-Based Planning and Budgeting Process that incorporates technology requirements, data flows, data storage techniques, and data access points (see also Activity-Based Planning and Budgeting Process).

Activity Consumption Rate In the context of a cost object and one of the activities required by that cost object, the quantity of the activity (number of occurrences) required to complete one unit of the cost object, measured in the unit of measure of the activity.

Activity Driver* The best single quantitative measure of the frequency and intensity of the demands placed on an activity by cost objects or other activities. It is used to assign activity costs to cost objects or to other activities.

Activity Requirement The quantity (number of occurrences) of an activity required to meet the total quantity of demand. Mathematically expressed, it is the sum of the demand of each cost object times its associated activity consumption rate (($Demand_1$ x Activity Consumption $Rate_1$) + ($Demand_2$ x Activity Consumption $Rate_2$) + ... ($Demand_n$ x Activity Consumption $Rate_n$)). (See also Activity Consumption Rate).

Buffer Capacity (See Excess Capacity)

Capacity* The physical facilities, personnel, and process available to meet the product or service needs of customers. Capacity generally refers to the maximum output or producing ability of a machine, a person, a process, a factory, a product, or a service (see also Capacity Management and Excess Capacity).

Capacity Management* The domain of cost management that is grounded in the concept that capacity should be understood, defined, and measured for each level in the organization to include market segments, products, processes, activities, and resources. In each of these applications, capacity is defined in a hierarchy of idle, non-productive, and productive views. (For further information see the CAM-I capacity model in Klammer 1996.)

Cascading Closed-Loop Models Closed-Loop Models for business units that have demand information flowing from the consumer unit to the supplier unit. A prerequisite to having Networked Closed-Loop Models (see also Closed-Loop Model, Consumer Units, Networked Closed-Loop Models, and Supplier Units).

Closed-Loop Model An activity-based budgeting algorithm that achieves operational balance (Stage 1), then financial balance (Stage 2), and which explicitly matches resource demand and resource capacity (see also Financial Balance, Operational Balance, and Resource Capacity).

Common Costs Costs incurred to support multiple cost objects that are not directly traceable to such objects in a specific time period.

Consumer Units Organizational units that acquire or use the goods or services of other units. This includes both internal and external business relationships and may exist in a hierarchical fashion, e.g. parent company and subsidiary and/or in a parallel fashion, e.g. information technology and human resource functions. (See also Supplier Units.)

Cost Driver* Any situation or event that causes a change in the consumption of a resource, or influences quality or cycle time. An activity may have multiple cost drivers. Cost drivers do not necessarily need to be quantified; however, they strongly influence the selection and magnitude of activity drivers and resource drivers. See also Activity Driver and Resource Driver.

Cost Management* The management and control of activities and drivers to calculate accurate product and service costs, improve business processes, eliminate waste, influence cost drivers, and plan operations. The resulting information will have utility in setting and evaluating an organization's strategies.

Cost Object* Any product, service, customer, contract, project, process, or other work unit for which a separate cost measurement is desired.

Direct Cost* A cost that can be directly traced to a cost object since a direct or repeatable cause-and-effect relationship exists. A direct cost uses a direct assignment or cost causal relationship to transfer costs. (See also Cost Object, Indirect Cost, and Tracing).

Excess Capacity The amount of capacity of a particular resource that is not used in a given period. Excess Capacity consists of Idle Capacity and unused Buffer Capacity. Idle Capacity is the broad term for all capacity that is not used, excluding that which is required to buffer processes (Buffer Capacity).

Used Capacity consists of productive capacity and non-productive capacity. Buffer Capacity represents capacity that may be required in the normal course of business to accommodate short-term variations in processes, demands, and/or linked resources. It may or may not be actually used. Buffer Capacity must be optimized to business requirements and, as such, the cost of buffer capacity is included in the definition of product/service cost.

However, Idle Capacity is generally not desirable, representing capacity available but unexpectedly not used; therefore, its cost is generally excluded from product/service cost. Idle Capacity is particularly problematic if it is expected to recur over a longer period of time.

These terms are more fully explained in Klammer 1996.

(See also, Capacity).

Financial Balance A financial plan that builds on a balanced Operational Plan and delivers the required financial results (e.g., return on sales, absolute profitability). By definition, if the predicted financial results fail to meet the required financial results, the plan cannot be financially balanced but remains in Operational Balance. (See also Financial Plan, Operational Balance, and Operational Plan).

Financial Plan The result of Stage 2 of the Closed-Loop Model. A Financial Plan may or may not be in Financial Balance (see also Financial Balance).

Fixed Cost A cost that does not change materially in the planning period in response to changes in requirements. Property taxes on a building are an example of a fixed cost.

Formal Budget A document with the proper executive approval that includes sufficient detail of organization resources, including labor, non-labor, and statement of work forecasts, to represent an organization's strategic and operational plan for the upcoming business period, frequently one year. Formal budgets may be based on an activity-based approach, a traditional approach, or some combination of the two. However, formal budgets may be created independently of the actual calculation approach.

Government Cost Recovery Agency A government organization that provides products/services to customers and collects a fee to offset some or all of the costs. Some, but not all, of these organizations also receive legislative subsidies that are intended to mitigate the cost of products/services to customers.

Government Program Agency A government organization funded wholly or primarily through appropriation processes, and therefore does not charge a material fee for its services.

Indirect Cost* A resource or activity cost that cannot be directly traced to a final cost object since no direct or repeatable cause-and-effect relationship exists. An indirect cost uses an assignment or allocation to transfer costs (see also Direct Cost).

Idle Capacity (See Excess Capacity)

Networked Closed-Loop Models A Closed-Loop Model architecture where the financial and operational results of the Supplier Units' Closed-Loop Models are automatically fed into the Closed-Loop Models of the Consumer Units. Note that Cascading Closed-Loop Models are a prerequisite to Networked Closed-Loop Models (see also Cascading Closed-Loop Models, Closed-Loop Models, Consumer Units, and Supplier Units).

Operational Balance An operational plan is one that provides sufficient resource capacity to meet the sum of all demands placed on the organization, with an acceptable level of unused capacity (see Excess Capacity for definition of Unused Capacity, and Operational Plan).

Operational Plan The result of Stage 1 of the Closed-Loop Model. An Operational Plan may or may not be in Operational Balance (see Operational Balance).

Performance Measures* Indicators of the work performed and the results achieved in an activity, process, or organizational unit. Performance measures are both non-financial and financial. Performance measures enable periodic comparisons and benchmarking.

Process A series of activities that are linked to complete a specific output. A process has a beginning, an end, an output, and at least one clearly identified input.

Process Analysis Identifying, documenting, and studying the activities that generate a process, usually for the purpose of improving the process.

Resources* Economic elements applied or used in the performance of activities or to directly support cost objects. They include people, materials, supplies, equipment, technologies, and facilities.

Resource Capacity The quantity of each type of resource available in a given time period.

Resource Consumption Rate In the context of an activity and one of the resources required by that activity, the quantity of the resource required to complete one unit of the activity, measured in the unit of measure of the resource.

Resource Driver* The best single quantitative measure of the frequency and intensity of demands placed on a resource by other resources, activities, or cost objects. It is used to assign resource costs to activities, cost objects, or to other resources.

Resource Requirement The quantity of a resource required to meet the total quantity of demand, coming through activities. Mathematically expressed, it is the sum of the demand of each activity times its associated resource consumption rate ((Activity Requirement$_1$ x Resource Consumption Rate$_1$) + (Activity Requirement$_2$ x Resource Consumption Rate$_2$) + ... (Activity Requirement$_n$ x Resource Consumption Rate$_n$)). (See also Resource Consumption Rate).

Revenue Forecast The expression of a demand volume forecast in terms of the unit of currency of the organization.

Service Level Agreement A written agreement between a shared service provider and a shared service consumer that specifies the amount, cost, and quality of the services that will be provided during the period (see also Shared Services).

Shared Services The separation of some or all supporting processes into a separate organization, which in turn treats those processes as its own core business.

Step Cost A cost that is constant for a volume of demand within a specified range, but that changes once demand volume moves outside that range.

Strategy The way that an organization positions and distinguishes itself from its competitors. It is the basic business approach an organization follows to meet its goals.

Supplier Units Organizational units that provide or sell goods or services to other units. This includes both internal and external business relationships and may exist in a hierarchical fashion, e.g. parent company and subsidiary and/or in a parallel fashion, e.g. information technology and human resource functions. (See also Consumer Units.)

Tracing* The practice of relating resources, activities, and cost objects using the drivers underlying their cost causal relationships. The purpose of tracing is to observe and understand how costs arise in the normal course of business operations.

Unused Capacity (See Excess Capacity)

Variable Cost A cost element that varies directly and proportionately with changes in cost drivers, such as volume of production.

Variance The difference between an actual and an expected result.

Bibliography

Amsler, B., J. Busby, and G. Williams. 1993. Combining Activity Based Costing and Process Mappings: A Practical Study. *Integrated Mfg. Systems,* 4 (4): 10-17.

_____. 1998. Companies Strait-Jacketed by Annual Budget Process. *Management Accounting (London)*, 76 (1): 10.

_____. 1994. Enterprise-Wide Budgeting Demands Flexibility Beyond Spreadsheets. *Managing Office Technology,* 39 (2): 40-41.

Ansari, S., J. Bell, and T. Klammer. 1999. *Activity Based Budgeting, Modular Series: Management Accounting.* Boston, MA: Irwin/McGraw Hill.

Antos, J. A Better Way to Budget: Solving Traditional Budgeting Problems with ABB. Available at: www.bettermanagement.com/library/library.aspx?libraryid= 442&a=8.

Antos, J., and J. Brimson. 1999. Chapter 31: Activity Based Budgeting. In *Handbook of Budgeting,* Hoboken, NJ: John Wiley & Sons.

Ashworth, G., and H. Evans. 1995. Activity Based
Management - Moving Beyond Adolescence. *Management
Accounting (London)*, 73 (11): 26-30.

Barco, A. 1996. Asset-Based Budgeting for Facilities Support.
The Armed Forces Comptroller, 41 (2): 24.

Barkman, A. 1997. Synergy from A to Z, ABC to ZBB. *Journal
of Managerial Issues*, 9 (1): 54-71.

Birkin, F., and D. Woodward. 1997. Management
Accounting for Sustainable Development. *Management
Accounting (London)*, 75 (11): 40-42.

Bleiweiss, W. 1998. Measuring What Counts. *Telephony*, 235
(14): 50-52.

Block, R., and L. Carr. 1999. Activity Based Budgeting at
Digital Semiconductor. *International Journal of Strategic Cost
Management* (Spring): 17-31.

Borjesson, S. 1997. A Case Study on Activity Based
Budgeting. *Journal of Cost Management*, 10 (2): 7-18.

_____. 1994. What Kind of Activity Based Information
Does Your Purpose Require? *International Journal of
Operations & Production Management*, 14 (12): 79-99.

Bossidy, L., and R. Charan. 2002. *Execution: The Discipline of
Getting Things Done*. New York, NY: Random House Inc.

Brimson, J., J. Antos, S. Player, and J. Collins. 1998. *Driving Value Using Activity Based Budgeting*. Hoboken, NJ: John Wiley & Sons.

Brimson, J., and R. Fraser. 1991. The Key Features of ABB. *Management Accounting (London)*, 69 (1): 42-43.

Brockhoff, K., and A. Chakrabarti. 1997. Take a Proactive Approach to Negotiating Your R&D Budget. *Research Technology Management*, 40 (5): 37-41.

Classe, A. 1995. Alphabet Soup. *Accountancy*, 116 (1227): 70-74.

Coburn, S., H. Grove, and T. Cook. 1997. How ABC Was Used In Capital Budgeting. *Management Accounting*, 78 (11): 38-46.

Cokins, G. 1996. *Activity-Based Cost Management: Making it Work*. New York, NY: McGraw-Hill, Inc.

_____. 1997. If Activity Based Costing is the Answer, What is the Question? *IIE Solutions*, 72 (3): 38-42.

_____. 1998. ABC Can Spell a Simpler, Coherent View of Costs. *Computing Canada*, 24 (32): 34.

_____. 1997. Chapter B8: Activity Based Budgeting. In James Edwards (ed.), *Handbook of Cost Management*. New York, NY: Warren, Gorman, and Lamont.

_____. New-Age Accounting: Activity Based Budgeting. Available at: www.bettermanagement.com/Library/Library.aspx?Libraryid=1250&a=8

_____. 1998. Why is Traditional Accounting Failing Managers? *Hospital Material Management Quarterly,* 20 (2): 72-80.

Connolly, T., and G. Ashworth. 1994. An Integrated Activity Based Approach to Budgeting. *Management Accounting (London),* 72 (3): 32.

Cooper, R., and R. Kaplan. 1992. Activity Based Systems: Measuring the Costs of Resource Usage. *Accounting Horizons,* 6 (3): 1-13.

_____. 1991. Chapter 11: Stage IV: Using ABC for Budgeting and Transfer Pricing. In *The Design of Cost Management Systems,* Englewood Cliffs, NJ: Prentice Hall.

_____. 1998a. Chapter 15. Stage IV: Using ABC for Budgeting and Transfer Pricing. In *Cost and Effect: Using Integrated Cost Systems to Drive Profitability and Performance,* Boston, MA: Harvard Business School Press.

_____. 1998b. The Promise - and Peril - of Integrated Cost Systems. *Harvard Business Review,* 76 (2): 109-119.

Cross, R., M. Majikes, and J. Kelleher. 1997. Activity Based Costing in Commercial Lending: The Case of Signet Bank. *Commercial Lending Review,* 12 (4): 24-30.

Dierks, P., and G. Cokins. 2000. *Glossary of Activity-Based Management.* Bedford, TX: CAM-I.

Dhavale, D. 1998a. Capacity Costs - A Perspective (Part 1). *International Journal of Strategic Cost Management,* 1 (1): 51-57.

_____. 1998b. Capacity Costs - A Perspective (Part 2). *International Journal of Strategic Cost Management,* 1 (2): 3-12

Drury, C. 1998. Management Accounting Information Systems in UK Building Societies. *The Service Industries Journal,* 18 (2): 125-143.

Ermer, D., and M. Kniper. 1998. Delighting the Customer: Quality Function Deployment for Quality Service Design. *Total Quality Management,* 10 (4/5): S86-S91.

Euske, K.J., N. Frause, T. Peck, B. Rosenteil, and S. Schreck. 1998. *Service Process Measurement: Breaking the Code.* Bedford TX: CAM-I.

Foster, T. 1999. Time to Learn the ABC's of Logistics. *Logistics Management and Distribution Report,* 38 (2): 67-70.

Franceschini, F., and S. Rossetto. 1998. Quality Function Deployment: How to Improve Its Use. *Total Quality Management*, 6 (9): 491-500.

Grasso, L. 1997. Is it Time to Revisit Zero-Based Budgeting? *Journal of Cost Management*, 10 (2): 22-29.

Gurowka, J. 1997. Activity Based Costing Software: The Market Explodes. *CMA,* 71 (4): 13-19.

Hansen, S., and W. A. Van der Stede. 2002. Six Facets of Budgeting: Antecedents and Performance. Working Paper, USC.

Harry, M., and R. Schroeder. 2000. *Six Sigma: The Breakthrough Management Strategy Revolutionizing the World's Top Corporations.* New York, NY: Doubleday.

Harvey, M. 1991. Activity Based Budgeting. *Certified Accountant.*

_____. 1991. Businesses Gain Competitive Edge with Activity Based Budgeting. *Certified Accountant.*

Henderson, I. 1997. Does Budgeting Have to Be So Troublesome? *Management Accounting (London),* 75 (9): 27.

Hope, J., and R. Fraser. 1997. Beyond Budgeting ... Breaking Through the Barrier to 'The Third Wave'. *Management Accounting (London),* 75 (11): 20-23.

_____. 1998. Managing Without Budgets: The European Experience. *Corporate Controller*, (Sept-Oct): 11-19.

_____. 2003. *Beyond Budgeting: How Managers Can Break Free from the Annual Performance Trap*. Boston, MA: Harvard Business School Press.

Innes, J., and F. Mitchell. 1997. The Application of Activity Based Costing in the United Kingdom's Largest Financial Institutions. *The Service Industries Journal (London)*, 17 (1): 190-203.

_____. 1996. ABC: A Follow-Up Survey of CIMA Members. *Management Accounting (London)*, 74 (7): 50-51.

Kaplan, R. and D. Norton. 2001. *The Strategy Focused Organization*. Boston, MA: Harvard Business School Press.

Klammer, T. 1996. *Capacity Measurement & Improvement: A Manager's Guide to Evaluating and Optimizing Capacity Productivity*. Boston, MA: Irwin Professional Pub.

Kos, H., and W. McKinney. 1999. Walking the Talk: Implementing Real Activity Based Budgeting. Available at: www.bettermanagement.com/Library/Library.aspx?LibraryID=488 &a=8

Lindahl, F. 1997. Activity Based Costing Implementation and Adaptation. *Human Resource Planning,* 20 (2): 62-66.

Lynch, T., and C. Lynch. 1996. Twenty-First Century Budget Reform: Performance, Entrepreneurial, and Competitive Budgeting. *Public Administration Quarterly,* 20 (3): 255-284.

Mason, B. 1996. Activity Based Costing at Scottish Courage. *Management Accounting (London),* 74 (7): 32.

May, M. 1995a. Activity Based Management Accounting. *Management Accounting (London),* 73 (1): 40.

_____. 1995b. The Role of Management Accounting in Performance Improvement: Does Your Management Accounting System Support Empowerment? *Management Accounting (London),* 73 (4): 14.

_____. 1998. Advanced Activity Based Management Accounting *Management Accounting (London),* 76 (7): 32.

May, M., A. Rajguru, L. Burns, M. Howes, and G. Matthews. 1997. Preparing Organizations to Manage the Future. *Management Accounting (London),* 75 (2): 28-32.

McClenahen, J. 1995. Generally Accepted Practice: The Pluses and Minuses of Activity Based Budgeting. *Industry Week,* 244 (11): 13-14.

McLemore, I. 1997. The New Frontier in Budgets. *Business Finance* (Sept):32.

McNair, C. J., and The CAM-I Cost Management Integration Team. 2000. *Value Quest*. Bedford, TX: CAM-I.

Morris, H. 2002. Budgeting, Planning, and the Three Levels of Analytic Applications. *IDC Research Document* #28068.

Morrow, M. and G. Ashworth. 1994. An Evolving Framework for Activity Based Approaches. *Management Accounting (London)*, 72 (2).

Morrow, M. and T. Connolly. 1991. The Emergence of Activity Based Budgeting. *Management Accounting (London)*, 69 (2): 38-39.

Morrow, M. and M. Hazell. 1992. Activity Mapping and Business Process Redesign. *Management Accounting (London)*, 70 (2): 36-38.

Osborne, D., N. Ringrose. 1998. Market-Focused Cost Reduction. *Management Accounting (London)*, 76 (1): 28-30.

Player, S., and D. Keys. 1996. *Activity-Based Management: Arthur Andersen's Lessons from the ABM Battlefield*. New York, NY: MasterMedia, Ltd.

Project Management Institute. 2000. *A Guide to the Project Management Book of Knowledge*. Newtown, PA: Project Management Institute.

Pryor, T. 1999. What's Happened to ABB? Available at: www.icms.net/news-18.htm

Rathbone, H., and C. Lynn. 1998. The Planning Roundabout: Part One of a Five-Part Series *Management Accounting (London)*, 76 (11): 40.

_____. 1999. The Planning Roundabout: Part Two of a Five-Part Series. *Management Accounting (London)*, 77 (1): 24.

Sanders, S. 1995. Actively Informative Planning. *CPA Journal*, 65 (8): 66-68.

Sandison, D., S. Hansen, and R. Torok. 2003. Activity Based Planning and Budgeting: A Look at a New Approach from CAM-I. *Journal of Cost Management* (March/April): 16-22.

Schmidt, J. 1992. Is it Time to Replace Traditional Budgeting? *Journal of Accountancy (British)*, 174 (4): 103-107.

Schneeweiss, C. 1998. On the Applicability of Activity Based Costing as a Planning Instrument. *International Journal of Production Economics* 54: 277-284.

Segars, A., V. Grover, and J. Teng. 1998. Strategic Information Systems Planning: Planning System Dimensions, Internal Co-Alignment and Implications for Planning Effectiveness. *Decision Sciences*, 29 (2): 303-345.

Sharman, P. 1996. Activity / Process Budgets: A Tool for Change Management. *CMA*, 70 (2): 21-24.

_____. 1995. How to Implement Performance Measurement in Your Organization. *Management Accounting Magazine*, 69 (8): 38-42.

Sharman, P., H. Armitage, and R. Nicholson. 1993. Activity Based Costing Management: A Growing Practice. *Management Accounting Magazine*, 67 (2): 17-21.

Simons, R. 1995. *Levers of Control: How Managers Use Innovative Control Systems to Drive Strategic Renewal*. Boston, MA: HBS Press.

Smith, M. 1997. Putting NFI's to Work in a Balanced Scorecard Environment. *Management Accounting (London)*, 75 (3): 32-35.

Stevens, M. 2002. *Activity Based Planning and Budgeting Workshop*. New Bedford: TX, PCS Consulting and CAM-I.
Stevens, T. 1997. Balancing Act. *Industry Week*, 24 (6): 40-48.

Stratton, A., and W. S. McKinney. 1999. *An ABB Manager's Primer*. Beaverton, OR: ABC Technologies, Inc.

The Office of Management and Budget. 2002. *The President's Management Agenda, Section 5 – Goal to Link Results to Budget*, available at www.whitehouse.gov/omb/budget

Unruh, C., B. Voss, and J. Wells. 1994. Budgeting Moves to a New Dimension. *The Journal of Business Strategy*, 15 (2): 6-7.

Walker, M. 1992. Attribute Based Costing. *Australian Accountant*, 62 (2): 42-45.

_____. 1998. Attributes or Activities? Looking to ABCII. *Australian CPA*, 68 (9): 26-28.

Welch, J. and J. Byrne. 2001. *Jack: Straight from the Gut*. New York, NY: Warner Business Books.

White, T. 1997. *The 60 Minute ABC Book – Activity Based Costing for Operations Management*. Bedford, TX: Consortium for Advanced Manufacturing – International.

Wilhelmi, M. and B. Kleiner. 1995. New Developments in Budgeting. *Management Research News*, 18 (3-5): 78-87.

Index